WOMEN
OF
PURPOSE

Shared Identity Unique Calling

BY
SHARRI BURGGRAAF

ISBN:979-8-9903659-0-2 Paperback
LCCN Control Number - 2024906849

FORWARD

Do you know yourself? Or the someone others think you are? Does it seem that there may be parts of yourself that you have never known?

Imagine looking down a long hallway with many doors on each side. Would you be curious, thinking, I want to know what is written on each door and what is inside the room? What does it have to do with you?

Then suddenly the idea goes through you: These are facets of the jewel you were made to be; indeed who you are if only you will allow the doors to be opened.

Would this frighten you? Excite you? Be hard to shake off?

This book which you hold in your hands (or are seeing through this screen) will help you to open doors and develop the ability to believe and grow in what you come to know about yourself. You may have even peeked into a few doors but rejected what you saw because you didn't know what to do with what you discovered

Sound too good to be true? The person Sharri Burggraaf has become is so far beyond what her circumstances would have caused you to believe possible. Now is the time to be led through the process God has led her through.

He wants us to be all that He created us to be. We are His workmanship, and He knows the way for us to go to more fully be a woman of purpose. His love never fails.

I only met Sharri a few years ago and she had already gone through a lot of what is described in this book. She is now in the position to carry out the assignments God gave her to do. Come and see the goodness of God! Come and meet more of the woman of purpose He created you to be.

Laurie Simerson is the author and illustrator of "The Adventures of T & T," a parable that teaches important life lessons through the story of two ostriches named Tanglefoot and Tumblewood who choose to follow God's guidance on their adventure. As a fellow author who understands the journey of discovering God's purpose, she served as an editor for this book, ensuring its message honors God while speaking clearly to women seeking their calling—and was deeply inspired by the material. She has valuable spiritual insight and helps to lead a prayer ministry where she resides in California.

★★★★★
"This book is a lifeline for survivors and truth-seekers alike."
~ Laura M., trauma recovery advocate
Sharri Burggraaf has written a deeply healing and biblically rooted guide for women navigating identity, trauma, and purpose. As a survivor myself, I found her words to be both validating and empowering. Her courage to speak truth, especially on hard topics like gender and false identity, has given me language for what I've struggled to explain. I felt seen, known, and guided back to Jesus on every page.

★★★★★
"Biblical truth, spiritual strength, and soul-level clarity."
~Denise R., pastor's wife and women's ministry leader
This is more than a book; it's a discipleship tool, a personal devotional, and a healing journey all in one. Sharri weaves Scripture, reflection, and personal testimony in a way that challenges and encourages at the same time. I will be using this in our women's groups for years to come. Every woman needs to read this.

★★★★★
"A must-read for women longing to live fully and fearlessly in Christ."
~Joy L., Christian counselor
What sets Women of Purpose apart is Sha~rri's authenticity. She writes from lived experience—raw and redemptive. Her insights into spiritual warfare, identity distortion, and our Kingdom calling are delivered with compassion and authority. This is not fluff. It's Spirit-led truth that changes lives.

*Sharri's **"Women of Purpose"** is a rich resource of scripture, reflections, and affirmations that support the spiritual growth of women of faith.*
~ Lyn Barrett, MEd, MDiv Author, Memoir Coach, Founder of Dissociative Writers
With Women of Purpose as your guide, may your true self emerge through God's grace.

DEDICATED TO

Jesus Christ, my Savior, Lover and Healer of my broken heart, my mind, body & soul.

Frank, my husband of 32 years, my best friend and greatest supporter. You have loved me through the most challenging times and showed me a man's love, preparing me to receive the perfect love of God the Father so I could accept Jesus.

My children, Tina, Jay, and Lisa who have become my friends and siblings in Christ. I'm proud to be your mom. My grandchildren and great-grandchildren, and to Ava, one of my greatest encouragers. I'm proud to be your Nana. You're all precious.

Tina, thank you for being the first one in our family who saw the elephant in the room and dared to break the cycle of abuse as I did. Your faith has inspired me.

Aunt Minnie, your prayers were answered. I thank you for every prayer and letter.

Gail, the friend God sent when my children and I needed her to keep me alive and to start my journey to do more than just survive.

Shirley, Samara, Stephanie, and Suzy, friends and sisters who love and believe me.

The Saturday Trauma Reboot and Bible study ladies who have become close friends and sisters in Christ—Sue, Wendy, Tina, Sharon, and Cheri —thank you for walking through this book with me to help make it even better.

Laura Ballard, my friend and spiritual mentor, who gave me a tribe of sisters in Christ that became true family, and who opened her home as a place where I could once again worship, in Spirit and in Truth.

Fern and Audrey, formerly with Discovering MErcy, who taught me to walk from fear into love and gave me hope to break free from satanic ritual abuse, mind control and trafficking starting as a young girl.

My friend Freidel, who has shown such kindness and compassion. Together we have grown and healed so much and have proven that help exists.

Laurie, my friend and sweet sister in Christ, my Monday share-and-prayer partner who introduced me to the name Yeshua HaMashiach and helped edit and make revisions to this book.

Lyn Barrett, owner of Dissociative Writers and my writing mentor, author of Crazy: Reclaiming Life from the Shadow of Traumatic Memory, your guidance has been invaluable. I have grown in countless ways because of you.

My many survivor friends, peer supporters, and the thousands who have engaged with my blog, podcast, YouTube and TikTok channels and videos over the past six years. I pray for your healing and freedom!

My therapists; especially Caleb and Crystal who encouraged me to focus on my wins—prayer ministers Liv and Andrea, who have been instrumental in my spirtual healing journey from surviver to overcomer—warrior women, Cindy Metcalf, Buffy, Anastasia, author Katy Lee, amazing, bold, and courageous, trailblazing women.

All those unnamed but deeply appreciated—your support, love, and faith have been integral to my journey of recovery. You are truly gifts from God.

ABOUT THE AUTHOR

Sharri Burggraaf is a wife, mother, and Nana who was rescued by Jesus Christ from the captivity of ritual abuse, mind control, and sex trafficking that began in early childhood. An overcomer with nearly 40 years of lived experience in recovery, she is a passionate advocate—both for herself and for others, raising awareness about the link between multi-generational abuse and sex trafficking an advocate and activist, a catylst for change.

She is the founder of S.H.O.U.T. (Survivors Helping Others Unite Together) for Help Inc., a nonprofit through which she organized a national three-day conference in the 1990s in Des Moines, Iowa. Sharri runs a website titled Arise and Shine After Abuse.

As a writer and speaker, she has shared her story and insight at numerous conferences on healing from RAMCOA (Ritual Abuse, Mind Control, and Organized Abuse). She authors a blog, hosts a podcast, TikToks and creates YouTube content to minister to survivors, therapists, and supporters. She volunteers for Relentless Hope coordinating speakers for support groups, podcast co-host, and is writing a training titled, "Project J.U.S.T.I.C.E." for clinicians, clergy, law enforcement, hospitals and others who support survivors in hopes they can be helped and have the hope that she has found in Jesus Christ.

As a leader, Sharri facilitates trauma-recovery classes for women—empowering, equipping, and encouraging them to find their voice, write their story, and break the silence of shame. She has led writing workshops designed specifically for individuals with dissociative identities since 2019. A song writer, she has produced 7 albums with the name "Unchained Sacred Echo" as her contribution to survivors and those needing the freedom with the hope of healing her own songs brought her.

She views (Dissociative Identity Response) as a miraculous coping mechanism given by God, not a disorder by which a child can psychologically "go away" during unspeakable trauma in order to survive until they are strong enough to heal.

Over the years, Sharri has helped thousands of survivors by validating their experiences, offering support through recovery, and reminding them of their inherent worth and value as human beings. Her message is one of transformation through the love of God and hope and healing through a personal relationship with Jesus Christ.

She shares how God's love brought her from religion to relationship—not through rules or traditions, but through grace. Once filled with self-hatred and condemnation, she now lives in acceptance and self-love grounded in her identity in Christ.

As a disciple called to reach the nations, Sharri teaches women to discover their purpose, shared identity, and unique calling—so they can live fully as the beautifully created women God made them to be: followers of Christ who live in the world but are not conformed to it.

She is also the creator of faith-based tools such as affirmation cards, the Who I Am in Christ and the Names of God poster—all designed to affirm secure identity and reveal the true character of God.   www.ariseandshineafterabuse.com

GloryGraafics Etsy Shop
https://glorygraafics.etsy.com

For God so loved

_____

that He gave His only begotten Son so that whosoever believes in Him shall not perish but have everlasting life. John 3:16

Table of Contents

A Note From the Author

I speak to you as a woman who has experienced deep healing after a lifetime of extreme abuse. For many years, I thought I would never make it to the other side of the darkness and evil that had stolen so much from my life. But God had other plans. He already knew the future He had prepared for me—a future filled with hope, though it would take several decades for me to truly grasp it.

After my father died in 1984, I began experiencing unrelenting tears, nightmares, flashbacks, and overwhelming terror. These memories, long buried by my mind, suddenly began to surface. What I had once blocked from my conscious awareness now threatened to consume me. But God, in His mercy, created our minds to protect us in times of unbearable trauma. Some call it Dissociative Identity Disorder. I believe it is a miraculous gift from God—a way for a child to survive when nothing else could protect her.

During a trip to the Ark Encounter and the Creation Museum—while struggling emotionally and physically—God spoke to me in an unexpected moment: "*I want you to be a mouthpiece for women and speak out for those who can't speak for themselves.*" As I looked up, I noticed a poster on the inside of the door featuring a woman speaker at an upcoming event. I cried out to God, "Lord, I'm such a mess. How can You possibly use me?" It took several more years before I began to see how He could. And He did. I am an overcomer, transformed because my life has been touched by Jesus Christ, the Healer of my soul. God has truly created beauty from ashes and revealed to me that my purpose is to share the hope I found through Jesus Christ and His redemptive healing power. Since that moment, I have launched a website, blog, podcast, and YouTube channel to share my story and raise awareness about ritual abuse, mind control, and trafficking.

I have spoken for Relentless Hope's fundraisers, and at An Infinite Mind's Healing Together Conference for three consecutive years.

With trafficking and child pornography being a multi-billion-dollar a year industry protected by powerful people, much evil continues to go undetected. Yet, God has called me to guide other women—to help them find their voice, their healing, their purpose, and their identity in Christ. To my sisters in Christ: God doesn't call the equipped—He equips the called. Your brokenness becomes your testimony. His light shines brightest through the cracks in the broken places. Just as He transformed my pain into purpose, He can reveal your unique calling and use your story to impact countless lives. United in His love, we become vessels of hope and healing—living proof that nothing is impossible with God. Your unique calling awaits. I encourage you to trust His perfect timing and transforming power and never never give up hope. His name is Jesus Christ.

QUOTES

God doesn't waste anything. He uses everything you've been through, good and bad, to shape the purpose He has for you. — **Ruth Chou Simons**

God has created you on purpose, for a purpose. Nothing about my birth - or yours was random or accidental. I was born for this time - and so were you. We were each chosen for a particular, cosmically important task that can be done by no one else. **~Christine Caine~**

When you know God, you'll find your purpose. **~Kay Arthur~**

When we feel fear, we have a choice—we can do it afraid! That's what courage is. True courage is moving forward in the face of fear.
~Joyce Meyer~

We will not be given a mission without the means to accomplish it. **~Beth Moore~**

God's plan is always the best. Sometimes the process is painful and hard. But don't forget that when God is silent, He's doing something for you.
~ Priscilla Shirer~

Your calling is found where your talents and burdens collide. **~Lysa TerKeurst~**

God is preparing you for what He has prepared for you. **~Christine Caine~**

In the midst of your battles, never forget that God loves you and He has a plan for you. God doesn't call the qualified. He qualifies the called. **~Joyce Meyer ~**

God will meet you where you are in order to take you where He wants you to go. **~Tony Evans~**

Your calling should be a megaphone for God's glory, not your own.
~Priscilla Shirer~

Your calling is not just about you; it's about how God wants to use you to impact others.
~Bianca Olthoff~

Your potential is the sum of all the possibilities God has for your life.
~Chrystal Evans Hurst ~

Your purpose is not a destination, it's a daily decision. **~Francis Chan~**

INTRODUCTION

When God created you, He called you into relationship with Himself. As believers in Christ, we share a foundational purpose: to know God intimately through Jesus Christ and to make Him known through discipleship. Yet within that shared purpose, God has given each of us a unique calling—crafted through our spiritual gifts, passions, and abilities. This personal calling becomes our individual expression of His Kingdom work.

By discovering our gifts, aligning our lives with Kingdom principles, and allowing the Holy Spirit to guide us, we can walk in the fullness of our divine calling—effectively building His Kingdom.

"So God created mankind in His own image, in the image of God He created them; male and female He created them." —**Genesis 1:27**

You reflect God's divine nature and character. As His daughter, you possess inherent dignity and worth. In a world that constantly pushes us to measure our value by achievements or outward success, God offers something far greater: an invitation to be fully known and deeply loved through relationship with Jesus, as His beloved bride.

With Jesus as our Bridegroom, we are free to submit and surrender not out of fear or obligation, but from a place of love and delight. As we serve Him, we experience the profound joy that intimacy with Him brings. This relationship becomes the foundation of our identity and the wellspring from which our purpose flows.

In biblical times, women were often treated as second-class citizens, facing significant social and legal restrictions. Yet Jesus broke cultural norms to uplift, honor, and dignify women. His interactions with them demonstrated unconditional love, acceptance, and compassion. He welcomed women as disciples, affirmed their spiritual gifts, and supported them emotionally in their suffering. He engaged the Samaritan woman at the well in deep spiritual conversation. He healed the woman with chronic bleeding and praised her faith. He comforted Martha and Mary in their grief, and protected the woman caught in adultery, choosing mercy over condemnation. Jesus demonstrated, time and again, that women are capable of deep spiritual insight, worthy of love, and called to walk in divine purpose.

Just as He spoke to those women, He desires to speak tenderly to you, reaching into the wounded places of your heart that you've hidden for protection. Your combination of gifts, experiences, and passions is not random; it is His intentional design. He created you to uniquely reflect His glory and expand His Kingdom.

In His presence, you will find fullness of joy, healing, and transformation. As you walk with Him, may you discover the beautiful place He's prepared for you in His grand plan.

"Your purpose is greater than your pain."

Myles Munroe

CHAPTER 1

What is a Woman of Purpose

HER DIVINE CHARACTER

"She is fearless and resolute, bold and unyielding; a trailblazer in every sense because the Lion of Judah roars within her and ignites her passion and desire for the Kingdom of God." Proverbs 28:1, Revelation 5:5, Romans 12:11

---◆---

✧ SHE IS ✧
FEARLESS · RESOLUTE · BOLD · UNYIELDING
COMPASSIONATE · LOVING · TENDER · FIRM
TRUSTWORTHY · TRUTHFUL · DETERMINED

She is unapologetically herself. She is compassionate and loving. **(Micah 6:8)**

Tender and gentle—yet strong. **(1 Peter 3:4)**

She knows how to be firm when it matters. **(Ecclesiastes 3:7–8)**

She is assertive, confident in her calling, and deeply aware of what God desires. **(Ephesians 2:10)**

Still, she's not afraid to ask Him for more. **(James 1:5, Hebrews 4:16)**

She is trustworthy, and in her is no deceit. **(Proverbs 12:22, Psalm 32:2)**

She speaks truth boldly in a world where truth is often rejected. **(Ephesians 4:25, John 8:32, Proverbs 31:26)**

She is a fearless leader with unwavering determination. **(Joshua 1:9, Galatians 6:9)**

She confronts life's challenges and faces trials with resolve and intention. **(Romans 5:3–5, James 1:12)**

She is victorious—not defined by her past, but healed from it—and she walks in the victory Christ died to give her. **(2 Corinthians 5:17, Romans 8:37, Revelation 12:11)**

She is an overcomer. **(1 John 5:4–5)**

She is more than a conqueror. **(Romans 8:37)**

"She is untameable as she fearlessly advances against the domain of darkness armed with the light, love, mercy, truth, and salvation of Almighty God." Ephesians 6:10–18, John 1:5, Romans 13:12, 2 Corinthians 10:4

HER KINGDOM IMPACT

"She is a formidable force for the Kingdom of God, advancing His truth and justice with unwavering conviction, defending the vulnerable and confronting injustice with divine purpose and authority." (Proverbs 31:8–9; Isaiah 1:17; Micah 6:8)

✦

◇ SHE IS ◇
UNMOVEABLE · UNDAUNTED · UNAFRAID
A RULE MAKER · A WORLD SHAKER
A HEART ENCOURAGER
A DEFENDER · A SUPPORTER · AN ADVOCATE

Her impact on the world is undeniable. She is playful, yet professional. She is unmoveable and will not stand for being exploited, manipulated, harassed, or bullied **(Psalm 62:6; Isaiah 54:17)**.

She is a rule maker, a world shaker, and a heart encourager because she is unsatisfied with the injustices in this world **(Amos 5:24; Romans 12:21)**.

She is a defender and supporter of orphans, widows, the poor in spirit, and those who are less fortunate or abused **(James 1:27; Matthew 5:3–10; Proverbs 31:20)**.

Guided by her divine calling, she navigates the complexities of life with grace and conviction **(Ephesians 4:1–3)**. She unashamedly puts herself out there with incredible courage and bravery, taking a stand for herself and others **(Joshua 1:9; Esther 4:14; Proverbs 31:25)**.

To the kingdom of darkness, she is a formidable force to be reckoned with, advocating for justice and truth in a world desperate for redemption **(John 1:5; Ephesians 5:11; Isaiah 60:1–2)**.

She is undaunted by the obstacles that stand in her way because she sees them as opportunities **(Romans 5:3–5; James 1:2–4)**.

"She embraces her limitless potential in Christ, unbound by worldly limitations." (Philippians 4:13; Ephesians 3:20; Colossians 3:2–3)

HER SPIRITUAL IDENTITY

"She stands unshakeable on the Solid Rock of Christ, unbounded by worldly limitations, embracing her divine identity as a cherished daughter of the Most High God." (Psalm 18:2; 1 Corinthians 3:11; Galatians 3:26; Romans 8:16–17)

✦

◇ SHE IS ◇
INTEGRATED · UNDIVIDED · UNCOMPROMISING
UNSHAKEABLE · UNDEFEATABLE · UNBOUNDED
WISE · FIRM · FAITHFUL

She is selflessly generous, pouring out her heart through her words, thoughts, and acts of love and kindness **(Proverbs 31:26; Galatians 5:13–14)**. She shares her resources freely **(Hebrews 13:16)**.

She is wise with God's wisdom **(James 3:17)**, firm in her faith **(1 Corinthians 16:13)**, and boldly shares about Jesus without hesitation **(Romans 1:16)**.

Embracing her journey of self-discovery, she transitions gracefully through the changing seasons of life **(Ecclesiastes 3:1; Philippians 4:11–13)**. She understands her role in shaping the world through Kingdom influence **(Matthew 5:14–16; Proverbs 31:25–26)**.

She stands apart from the world, rejecting its fleeting pursuits in favor of a life rooted in faith **(Romans 12:2; 1 John 2:15–17)**. She stands out because she does not conform to the world but is transformed by Christ **(2 Corinthians 5:17)**.

She is unbounded by worldly limitations **(Philippians 4:13)** and embraces her limitless potential in Him **(Ephesians 3:20)**.

She is integrated and undivided, walking in unity of mind and spirit **(1 Corinthians 1:10)**. She is uncompromising in her beliefs **(Ephesians 6:13–14)**.

She is unshakeable because her foundation is the Solid Rock—Jesus Christ **(Matthew 7:24–25)**. She is undefeatable, knowing that no weapon formed against her will prosper **(Isaiah 54:17)**.

"She is priceless. Her worth is of eternal significance, not worldly standards." (Proverbs 31:10; 1 Peter 3:3–4; Psalm 139:14)

HER DIVINE PURPOSE

"She walks with divine destiny, rare and distinctive in her calling, embracing her role as a Daughter of the Most High God with unwavering commitment to His purpose." (Jeremiah 29:11; Romans 8:28; 2 Timothy 1:9)

---✦---

✧ SHE IS ✧
UNCOMMON · RARE · DISTINCTIVE
DETERMINED · UNSTOPPABLE ·
FORWARD-FOCUSED
GOD-FOCUSED · UNDEFINABLE · BELOVED

She understands her role in the world and her place as a Daughter of the Most High God (**Galatians 4:7; Romans 8:16–17**). She is uncommon because she is deeply committed to God's will (**Romans 12:1–2**). She is rare, a distinctive presence in the Kingdom of God (**1 Peter 2:9**).

She is an inspiration to others, discipling them to pursue their own God-given purpose (**Matthew 28:19–20; Titus 2:3–5**). She embraces her God-given emotions without fear, channeling them toward understanding, growth, and empowerment (**Ecclesiastes 3:4; Proverbs 4:7**).

Her worth is of eternal significance, rooted not in worldly standards but in her intrinsic value as a cherished creation of God (**Psalm 139:13–14; 1 Peter 3:3–4**). She recognizes the need for new wineskins to hold the new wine (**Matthew 9:17**) and allows God to shape her into a vessel prepared for His truth and love (**2 Timothy 2:21**).

As she undergoes transformation, she aligns more fully with Jesus' example of compassion, humility, and grace (**Romans 12:2; Philippians 2:5–8**), reflecting His character in her daily walk.

She is determined to pursue Jesus (**Luke 9:23**). She is unstoppable, knowing that with God, nothing is impossible (**Luke 1:37; Philippians 4:13**). She is forward-focused, aware that her destiny lies ahead—not in the past (Philippians 3:13–14). She is God-focused because her identity and purpose are firmly rooted in Him (**Acts 17:28; Colossians 3:2–3**).

She is undefinable by human limitations (**Isaiah 55:8–9**). She is a beloved child of God (**Ephesians 1:4–6; Zephaniah 3:17**). She is priceless, chosen and precious in His sight (**Isaiah 43:4; 1 Peter 2:4–5**).

"She is unleashed because the power of God is at work in her life and the lives of others." (Ephesians 3:20; 2 Corinthians 4:7; Acts 1:8)

HER JOURNEY FROM GLORY TO GLORY

And we all, with unveiled face, beholding the glory of the Lord, are being transformed into the same image from one degree of glory to another. - 2 Corinthians 3:18

◇ SHE IS ◇
AUTHENTIC · TRANSPARENT · UNMASKED
HUMBLE · STEADFAST · UNMOVEABLE
UNLEASHED · UNASHAMED · UNSTOPPABLE

She is understated as a humble servant despite her remarkable achievements (**Matthew 23:11–12**). She is undone by God's love, grace, mercy, and forgiveness (**Ephesians 2:4–5; Psalm 103:8–12**).

She is feminine and secure in her identity in Christ (**Galatians 3:26–28**). She is unimpressed by the opinions of others because she knows who she is and to whom she belongs (**Ephesians 1:4–5; 1 Peter 2:9**). She is committed to fulfilling her part in God's grand plan (**Jeremiah 29:11; Romans 8:28**).

She moves at God's pace, refusing to be rushed by the world (**Ecclesiastes 3:1; Isaiah 40:31**). She has "God-fidence" because she trusts completely in the Lord, leans not on her own understanding, and acknowledges Him in all her ways (**Proverbs 3:5–6**).

She strides confidently, unencumbered by societal expectations (**Romans 12:2**). She is unphased by persecution or slander (**Matthew 5:11–12; 1 Peter 4:14**). She emerges stronger after every challenge and trial (**James 1:2–4; Romans 5:3–5**).

She is content and surprisingly satisfied (**Philippians 4:11–13**). She is authentic, transparent, unmasked, vulnerable, and real (**2 Corinthians 12:9–10; Psalm 34:18**).

She is humble, unswayed by earthly positions, possessions, or acceptance (**Philippians 3:7–8; 1 John 2:15–17**). She is steadfast in her faith (**1 Corinthians 15:58**) and faces adversity with unwavering fortitude (**Isaiah 41:10; Romans 8:37**).

"In her journey of purpose, she becomes who God created her to be - a radiant force of His love, truth, and power." (Ephesians 5:8; Colossians 3:10; Isaiah 60:1)

HER VICTORIOUS LEGACY

"She walks with unveiled face, transformed by His glory, authentically reflecting Christ's character as she moves from one degree of glory to another." (2 Corinthians 3:18)

◆

◇ SHE IS ◇
GUIDED · UNMOVEABLE · RESOLUTE
A BEACON · A FORCE · AN INSPIRATION
UNTAMEABLE · UNASHAMED · VICTORIOUS

She dares greatly because she knows her authority in Christ (**Luke 10:19; Ephesians 2:6**), and she boldly confronts the enemy declaring, "Nope, not today" (**James 4:7**). She is positive, aligning her thoughts with the mind of Christ (**Philippians 4:8; 1 Corinthians 2:16**). She speaks with grace, not criticism, and refuses to engage in gossip or slander (**Ephesians 4:29; Proverbs 16:28**). She remains informed enough about the world to avoid being consumed by it (**Romans 12:2; 1 John 2:15–17**), and she is engaged with the needs of those around her without casting judgment (**Matthew 7:1–2; Galatians 6:1–2**). She trades worldly pursuits for a life found in Christ (**Colossians 3:1–3**). She recognizes her potential and faces the unknown unafraid, trusting God with her future (**Jeremiah 29:11; Isaiah 41:10**). She motivates, encourages, and inspires (**1 Thessalonians 5:11**). She embraces her part in God's divine plan with unwavering commitment (**Romans 12:1–2; Ephesians 2:10**). She radiates the love of Jesus and shines her light brighter with every step (**Matthew 5:14–16; John 13:34–35**).

She is a force for change and renewal, untameable as she fearlessly advances against the domain of darkness (**Ephesians 6:10–12; 1 John 4:4**), armed with the light, love, mercy, truth, and salvation of Almighty God (**Psalm 27:1; John 1:5; Ephesians 2:4–5**) and the authority she holds through Jesus Christ (**Romans 8:37; Mark 16:17–18**).

She is a proponent of truth and justice in a world yearning for redemption (**Isaiah 1:17; Micah 6:8; John 8:32**).

The woman of purpose is every soul who embraces their calling, united in glorifying God before the triumphant return of Christ. (Titus 2:13; Revelation 19:7–8)

"Your purpose isn't measured by accomplishments, but by *alignment with God's heart.*"

Ann Voskamp

CHAPTER 2

Women of Purpose in the Bible

WOMEN OF PURPOSE IN THE BIBLE

God, in His infinite wisdom and love, created women for specific purposes and roles within His divine plan for Kingdom advancement. Throughout Scripture, women played pivotal roles, serving as powerful examples of faith, courage, and purpose—demonstrating their unique contributions and spiritual gifts **(Genesis 1:27; Ephesians 2:10)**.

These ordinary women were used in extraordinary ways at critical moments in history. Though they may not have felt equipped, God equips those He calls to fulfill His redemptive purposes **(Exodus 4:10–12; 1 Corinthians 1:27–29)**. This study highlights six such women:

◇ **Deborah** – Leadership **Judges 4–5** Deborah, a prophetess and judge, led Israel with wisdom and courage. Her leadership reflects bold faith and unwavering obedience to God in the face of battle.

◇ **Ruth** – Faithfulness **Ruth 1–4** Ruth's loyalty to Naomi and trust in God led to divine provision and redemption. Her story reveals steadfast love, humility, and God's faithfulness to those who follow Him.

◇ **Lydia** – Hospitality **Acts 16:13–15, 40** A businesswoman and worshiper of God, Lydia opened her heart and home to the early church. Her hospitality and generosity played a key role in supporting Paul's ministry.

◇ **Mary** – Motherhood **Luke 1:26–38; John 19:25–27** Mary, the mother of Jesus, exemplified humility, surrender, and nurturing love. Chosen to carry the Savior, her obedience and courage set her apart as a vessel of divine purpose.

◇ **Priscilla** – Mentorship **Acts 18:24–26; Romans 16:3–5** Priscilla, alongside her husband Aquila, mentored and taught with clarity and authority. Her knowledge of Scripture and willingness to disciple others helped strengthen the early church.

◇ **Esther** – Courage **Esther 4:13–16; 7:3–4** Esther's bravery in the face of death saved her people. She trusted God's timing and calling, walking in faith to fulfill a divine purpose *"for such a time as this."*

As you reflect on these women, remember that God has uniquely created you with purpose **(Psalm 139:13–16; Jeremiah 1:5)**. Embrace your identity as a woman of purpose, knowing He has entrusted you with meaningful roles in His family **(Romans 12:6–8; 1 Peter 4:10–11)**.

Let their stories inspire you to embrace your own purpose with courage as you study about each woman . Use the space provided to reflect on how their gifts, faith, and Kingdom impact speak to your calling in Christ and journal about their contributions and purpose.

ESTHER

A WOMAN OF DIVINE PURPOSE & COURAGE

Esther's Journey from Orphan to Queen of Persia

Key Scripture Passages:

"Mordecai had brought up Hadassah, that is Esther, his uncle's daughter, for she had neither father nor mother. The young woman had a beautiful figure and was lovely to look at, and when her father and mother died, Mordecai took her as his own daughter." – Esther 2:7

"When the turn came for Esther... to go in to the king, she asked for nothing except what Hegai, the king's eunuch who had charge of the women, advised... And Esther found favor in the eyes of all who saw her... And the king loved Esther more than all the women, and she won grace and favor in his sight more than all the virgins, so that he set the royal crown on her head and made her queen instead of Vashti." – Esther 2:15-17

"For if you keep silent at this time, relief and deliverance will rise for the Jews from another place, but you and your father's house will perish. And who knows whether you have not come to the kingdom for such a time as this?" Then Esther told them to reply to Mordecai, "Go, gather all the Jews to be found in Susa, and hold a fast on my behalf, and do not eat or drink for three days, night or day. I and my young women will also fast as you do. Then I will go to the king, though it is against the law, and if I perish, I perish." – Esther 4:14-16

"Then Queen Esther answered, 'If I have found favor in your sight, O king, and if it please the king, let my life be granted me for my wish, and my people for my request. For we have been sold, I and my people, to be destroyed, to be killed, and to be annihilated.'" – Esther 7:3-4

"Queen Esther, the daughter of Abihail, and Mordecai the Jew, gave full written authority... The command of Esther confirmed these practices of Purim, and it was recorded in writing." – Esther 9:29, 32

ESTHER: WALKING IN DIVINE PURPOSE

"And who knows whether you have not come to the kingdom for such a time as this?" - Esther 4:14

Spiritual Gifts & Character Traits:

Reflect on how Esther exemplified the following qualities throughout her journey:

- Faith
- Courage
- Leadership
- Wisdom

Reflection Questions:

How did Esther's response to Mordecai demonstrate both her faith and her courage?

What role did preparation (fasting, planning) play in Esther fulfilling her purpose?

How did Esther's position as queen align with God's purpose for her life?

What can we learn from Esther about recognizing and stepping into our God-given purpose?

How does Esther's story demonstrate the importance of godly counsel (Mordecai) in fulfilling our purpose?

Personal Application & Prayer:

[Journal your thoughts about applying Esther's example to your own life and write a prayer about embracing courage and purpose]

Let Esther's example of fasting and prayer inspire your own journey of purpose. Her courage and faith—demonstrated even in the face of fear—saved her people and reflect a life fully committed to God. Consider how God may be positioning you *"for such a time as this"* in your own sphere of influence.

DEBORAH

A WOMAN OF LEADERSHIP & PROPHECY

Her Journey as Judge, Prophetess, and Military Leader

Key Scripture Passages:

"Now Deborah, a prophetess, the wife of Lappidoth, was judging Israel at that time. She used to sit under the palm of Deborah between Ramah and Bethel in the hill country of Ephraim, and the people of Israel came up to her for judgment." — Judges 4:4–5

"She sent and summoned Barak the son of Abinoam from Kedesh-naphtali and said to him, 'Has not the Lord, the God of Israel, commanded you, "Go, gather your men at Mount Tabor, taking 10,000 from the people of Naphtali and the people of Zebulun"?'" — Judges 4:6

"Barak said to her, 'If you will go with me, I will go, but if you will not go with me, I will not go.' And she said, 'I will surely go with you. Nevertheless, the road on which you are going will not lead to your glory, for the Lord will sell Sisera into the hand of a woman.'" — Judges 4:8–9

"Then sang Deborah and Barak the son of Abinoam on that day: 'That the leaders took the lead in Israel, that the people offered themselves willingly—bless the Lord!'" — Judges 5:1–2

"The villagers ceased in Israel; they ceased to be until I arose; I, Deborah, arose as a mother in Israel." — Judges 5:7

Deborah was a woman set apart—called by God to lead Israel during a time of national turmoil. As a judge, prophetess, and military leader, she held multiple roles of influence with wisdom and humility. Her courage and spiritual discernment made her a trusted voice among the people and a vital instrument in God's deliverance of Israel.

She sought and obeyed the voice of the Lord, called others to rise in courage, and modeled godly leadership without hesitation. Her story exemplifies bold obedience, prophetic insight, and unwavering faith. In every role she fulfilled, Deborah walked in her divine calling with conviction and strength—leading by example and empowering others to do the same.

DEBORAH: WALKING IN DIVINE LEADERSHIP

"The rulers ceased in Isra'el, they ceased, until you arose, D'vorah, arose a mother in Isra'el.."
- Judges 5:7 (C JB)

Spiritual Gifts & Character Traits:

Reflect on how Deborah exemplified the following qualities:

Wisdom and Discernment:

Prophecy:

Leadership:

Courage and Faith:

Reflection Questions:

How did Deborah's role as a judge demonstrate her leadership and wisdom?

In what ways did Deborah's faith impact the decisions she made as a prophetess and military leader?

How did Deborah's prophecy influence Barak's actions and the outcome of the battle?

What can we learn from Deborah about stepping up in times of crisis and leading with courage?

How does Deborah's story demonstrate the importance of trusting God's plan even when the path isn't clear?

Personal Application & Prayer:

[Journal your thoughts on applying Deborah's example to your life, focusing on leadership, prophecy, and courage. Write a prayer asking God for wisdom, courage, and the ability to lead with His guidance.]

Let Deborah's story of leadership and prophecy inspire you to rise to the call of God in your own life. Her courage, faith, and wisdom demonstrate how God equips His people to lead in times of difficulty and uncertainty. Reflect on how God may be calling you to step into leadership, trusting in His direction and purpose for your life.

RUTH

A WOMAN OF FAITHFUL LOVE

Her Journey from Moab to God's Redemptive Plan

Key Scripture Passages:

"But Ruth said, 'Do not urge me to leave you or to return from following you. For where you go I will go, and where you lodge I will lodge. Your people shall be my people, and your God my God. Where you die I will die, and there will I be buried. May the Lord do so to me and more also if anything but death parts me from you.'" — Ruth 1:16–17

"And Ruth the Moabite said to Naomi, 'Let me go to the field and glean among the ears of grain after him in whose sight I shall find favor.'" — Ruth 2:2

"And Boaz answered her, 'All that you have done for your mother-in-law since the death of your husband has been fully told to me, and how you left your father and mother and your native land and came to a people that you did not know before. May the Lord reward your work, and your wages be full from the Lord, the God of Israel, under whose wings you have come to seek refuge.'" — Ruth 2:11–12

"The Lord make the woman, who is coming into your house, like Rachel and Leah, who together built up the house of Israel." — Ruth 4:11

"So Boaz took Ruth, and she became his wife. And he went in to her, and the Lord gave her conception, and she bore a son. Then the women said to Naomi, 'Blessed be the Lord, who has not left you this day without a redeemer, and may his name be renowned in Israel!'" — Ruth 4:13–14

"And they named him Obed. He was the father of Jesse, the father of David." — Ruth 4:17

Ruth's story is a powerful testimony of steadfast love, courageous faith, and divine providence. As a Moabite widow, she could have returned to her former life—but instead, she chose to remain with Naomi and follow the God of Israel. Her loyalty and humility opened the door to unexpected redemption.

Through Ruth's commitment and obedience, God wove her into the lineage of King David and ultimately the Messiah, Jesus Christ. Her life reminds us that faithful love and quiet trust in God can shape eternal legacies.

Ruth's journey—marked by sacrifice, perseverance, and divine favor—invites each of us to trust God's redemptive plan, even when the path ahead is uncertain.

RUTH: WALKING IN FAITHFUL LOVE

"Your people shall be my people, and your God my God." - Ruth 1:16

Spiritual Gifts & Character Traits:

Consider how Ruth demonstrated these qualities throughout her journey:

Faithfulness:

Love:

Humility:

Servanthood:

Reflection Questions:

How did Ruth's decision to follow Naomi demonstrate both faith and courage?

What role did Ruth's character play in how she was received in Bethlehem?

How did Ruth's faithfulness to Naomi lead to her place in God's redemptive plan?

What can we learn from Ruth about loyalty and commitment in relationships?

How does Ruth demonstrate God's providence in the lives of those who trust Him?

Personal Application & Prayer:

[Journal your thoughts about applying Ruth's example to your own life and write a prayer about faithful love and commitment]

Let Ruth's example of steadfast love and unwavering faithfulness inspire your own journey to walk faithfully, love deeply, and trust the Lord wholeheartedly. Through her commitment to Naomi and trust in God, she became part of His redemptive plan. Consider how your own faithful choices might be part of God's larger purpose in God's greater story of redemption.

16

MARY

A WOMAN OF HUMBLE OBEDIENCE

Her Journey as the Mother of Jesus

Key Scripture Passages:

"In the sixth month the angel Gabriel was sent from God to a city of Galilee named Nazareth, to a virgin betrothed to a man whose name was Joseph, of the house of David. And the virgin's name was Mary." — **Luke 1:26-27**

"And he came to her and said, 'Greetings, O favored one, the Lord is with you!' But she was greatly troubled at the saying, and tried to discern what sort of greeting this might be." — **Luke 1:28-29**

"And Mary said, 'Behold, I am the servant of the Lord; let it be to me according to your word.'" — *Luke 1:38*

"And Mary said, 'My soul magnifies the Lord, and my spirit rejoices in God my Savior, for he has looked on the humble estate of his servant. For behold, from now on all generations will call me blessed.'" — *Luke 1:46-48*

"But Mary treasured up all these things, pondering them in her heart." - Luke 2:19
"And his mother said to him, 'Son, why have you treated us so? Behold, your father and I have been searching for you in great distress.' And he said to them, 'Why were you looking for me? Did you not know that I must be in my Father's house?'" — *Luke 2:48-49*

MARY: WALKING IN DIVINE PURPOSE

"Behold, I am the servant of the Lord; let it be to me according to your word." - Luke 1:38

Spiritual Gifts & Character Traits:

Consider how Mary demonstrated these qualities throughout her journey:

Humility:

Faith:

Obedience:

Wisdom:

Reflection Questions:

How did Mary's immediate response to Gabriel demonstrate her faith and character?

What do we learn from Mary in trusting God's plan even when it seems impossible?

How did Mary's role as Jesus' mother require both strength and surrender?

What does Mary's magnificat (Luke 1:46-55) reveal about her understanding of God?

How can Mary's example of "treasuring things in her heart" guide our own spiritual reflection?

Personal Application & Prayer:

[Journal your thoughts about applying Mary's example to your own life and write a prayer about humble obedience to God's calling]

Let Mary's example of humble surrender and faithful obedience inspire your own journey with God. Through her willingness to say "yes" to God's unexpected plan, she participated in the greatest story ever told. Consider how God might be calling you to trust Him with your own future.

18

PRISCILLA

A WOMAN OF TEACHING & DISCIPLESHIP

Her Journey as a Teacher and Church Leader

Key Scripture Passages:

"He began to speak boldly in the synagogue, but when Priscilla and Aquila heard him, they took him aside and explained to him the way of God more accurately." — **Acts 18:26**

"After this Paul left Athens and went to Corinth. And he found a Jew named Aquila, a native of Pontus, recently come from Italy with his wife Priscilla, because Claudius had commanded all the Jews to leave Rome." — **Acts 18:1-2**

"Greet Prisca and Aquila, my fellow workers in Christ Jesus, who risked their necks for my life, to whom not only I give thanks but all the churches of the Gentiles give thanks as well." —

Romans 16:3-4

"The churches of Asia send you greetings. Aquila and Prisca, together with the church in their house, send you hearty greetings in the Lord." — **1 Corinthians 16:19**

"Greet Prisca and Aquila, and the household of Onesiphorus." - **2 Timothy 4:19**

And Paul stayed many days longer and then took leave of the brothers and set sail for Syria, and with him Priscilla and Aquila." — **Acts 18:18**

This verse shows her commitment to missionary work alongside Paul.

"And they devoted themselves to the apostles' teaching and the fellowship, to the breaking of bread and the prayers... And day by day, attending the temple together and breaking bread in their homes, they received their food with glad and generous hearts" — **Acts 2:42,46**

PRISCILLA: WALKING IN TEACHING MINISTRY

"...they took him aside and explained to him the way of God more accurately." — Acts 18:26

Spiritual Gifts & Character Traits:

Consider how Priscilla demonstrated these qualities throughout her ministry:

Teaching:

Hospitality:

Leadership:

Discernment:

Reflection Questions:

How did Priscilla's and Aquila demonstrate the power of partnership in service?

What does Priscilla's role in teaching Apollos reveal about women's roles in the early church?

How did Priscilla's hospitality—hosting a church in her home—complement her teaching ministry?

What can we learn from Priscilla about balancing different areas of ministry?
How does Priscilla's example inspire us to use our gifts in teaching and mentoring others?

Personal Application & Prayer:

[Journal your thoughts about applying Priscilla's example to your own life and write a prayer about using your gifts to build up the church]

Let Priscilla's example of faithfulness—through her partnership with Aquila, her commitment to accurate teaching, and her role in shaping the early church—inspire your own ministry within your sphere of influence. How might God be calling you to teach and mentor others?

LYDIA
A WOMAN OF GENEROUS HEART

Her Journey as a Businesswoman and Church Pioneer

Key Scripture Passages:

"One who heard us was a woman named Lydia, from the city of Thyatira, a seller of purple goods, who was a worshiper of God. The Lord opened her heart to pay attention to what was said by Paul." — **Acts 16:14**

"And after she was baptized, and her household as well, she urged us, saying, 'If you have judged me to be faithful to the Lord, come to my house and stay.' And she prevailed upon us." — **Acts 16:15**

"So they went out of the prison and visited Lydia. And when they had seen the brothers, they encouraged them and departed." — **Acts 16:40**

"Day by day, attending the temple together and breaking bread in their homes, they received their food with glad and generous hearts, praising God and having favor with all the people." — **Acts 2:46-47**

"Contribute to the needs of the saints and seek to show hospitality." — **Romans 12:13**

And on the Sabbath day we went outside the gate to the riverside, where we supposed there was a place of prayer, and we sat down and spoke to the women who had come together." — **Acts 16:13** *(This verse provides important context for Lydia's conversion, showing she was already a seeker of God, gathering with other women for prayer.)*

Now the full number of those who believed were of one heart and soul, and no one said that any of the things that belonged to him was his own, but they had everything in common." — Acts 4:32 *(This verse illustrates the type of Christian community Lydia helped establish through her generosity and hospitality.)*

LYDIA: WALKING IN BUSINESS AND MINISTRY

"The Lord opened her heart to pay attention to what was said by Paul." - Acts 16:14

Spiritual Gifts & Character Traits:

Consider how Lydia demonstrated these qualities throughout her journey:

Hospitality:

Leadership:

Generosity:

Discernment:

Reflection Questions:

How did Lydia's conversion demonstrate God's initiative and her responsive heart?

What role did Lydia's business success play in her ability to support the early church?

How did Lydia's hospitality create opportunities for the gospel to spread?

What can we learn from Lydia about using our professional positions and resources for God's purposes and Kingdom work?

Personal Application & Prayer:

[Journal your thoughts about applying Lydia's example to your own life and write a prayer about using your resources for God's kingdom]

Let Lydia's example of generous hospitality and business leadership inspire your own journey. Through her open heart and open home, she helped establish the early church in Europe. Consider how God might be calling you to use your resources and influence to advance His kingdom.

CHAPTER 3

False Identities

THE FALSE FOUNDATIONS OF IDENTITY

While we have an incredible identity in Christ, our natural human tendency is to search for identity in external things. Although these aspects may feel sturdy and reliable, anchoring our identity in them can ultimately lead to disappointment. None of them offer lasting security or stability, and they are not true measures of who we are in Christ. "*Those who cling to worthless idols turn away from God's love for them.*" **– Jonah 2:8** "*For you died, and your life is now hidden with Christ in God.*" **– Colossians 3:3**

External things we often base our identity on:

- Career/job title, academic achievements, financial success, skills
- Parental role (especially for women)
- Sports/athletic ability/physical fitness/appearance, health
- Social media presence/following, relationships/friends
- House, material possessions, family name
- Volunteer positions/community or church roles, activities
- Reputation or what others think of us
- Cultural or national identity, heritage
- Age (youth or experience)
- Political affiliation, group memberships

Personal Identity Assessment:

1. Circle any items in the list you may have found your identity in.
2. What would happen to your sense of self if what you circled were suddenly taken away?
3. Think of a time when you lost one of these. How did it affect your sense of who you are?

If we lose any of these external things, we may begin to question who we are without them and feel as if we've lost our identity. This loss can manifest as:

- Lack of confidence in our own skin and/or people pleasing
- Trying to look like we have it all together; perfectionism
- Living with a shifting, false identity based on how we want to be seen

"*People look at the outward appearance, but the Lord looks at the heart.*" **– 1 Samuel 16:7**

WHAT'S YOUR IDENTITY ROOTED IN

We can discover what our identity is rooted in by asking, "*What do I find my success in?*"

For many women, "success" or a sense of purpose often looks like:

- Having a college degree
- Being in a relationship
- Having a successful career (working hard enough to get approval)
- Being thin enough, pretty enough, good enough, pleasing enough
- Being the perfect wife or mother
- Having the ideal home/family life
- Gaining social media validation or popularity
- Achieving financial independence
- Maintaining youthful appearance
- Balancing multiple roles flawlessly
- Having well-behaved, successful children
- Being needed by others

Despite finding success in many areas, women often feel empty and insecure in these false identities. True fulfillment and security are not found in external achievements, but in the recognition that our identity is rooted in Christ.

Identity Root Assessment:

1. Look at the list above. Circle the items that you've pursued for validation or success.
2. Which of these pursuits leave you feeling most fulfilled?
3. Which leave you feeling most empty?

Quick Check: Consider these questions:

- Do I base my worth on my achievements or appearance?
  ☐ Yes ☐ No ☐ Sometimes
- Do I feel less valuable when I don't meet others' expectations?
  ☐ Yes ☐ No ☐ Sometimes
- Does my confidence depend on external validation?
  ☐ Yes ☐ No ☐ Sometimes

"What does it profit a man if he gains the whole world, yet loses his soul?" **– Mark 8:36**

THE FALSE IDENTITY OF CONFORMING

When we chase after the things of this world or seek our value in what society tells us we should be, we are not living from our true identity in Christ. Instead, we may be trying to conform to the people or things of this world. When we alter who we are depending on who is around, walking on eggshells to please others, we become conformers.

To identify areas where you may be conforming to external expectations or seeking approval, ask yourself the following questions:

- Are you allowing others to determine your identity? (approval seeking)
- Are you looking for validation because of insecurity?
- Are you a people pleaser?
- Do you change your identity to meet the expectations of others? (wearing a mask or false identity)

Conformity Assessment:

Check the behaviors that apply to you:

- ☐ Changing your opinion to match others in the room
- ☐ Dressing differently around certain people to fit in
- ☐ Hiding parts of your personality with specific groups
- ☐ Avoiding sharing your true thoughts or feelings
- ☐ Agreeing with others even when you disagree inside
- ☐ Sacrificing your needs to keep others happy
- ☐ Apologizing excessively for minor things
- ☐ Monitoring others' reactions to adjust your behavior
- ☐ Others (please specify)

Reflection Questions:

- In which relationships do you feel most tempted to conform? Why?
- What fears drive your conforming behaviors?
- What would it look like to be authentic in these situations?

The Bible instructs us not to conform to the things of this world:

Romans 12:2 - *"Do not be conformed to this world, but be transformed by the renewal of your mind, that by testing you may discern what is the will of God, what is good and acceptable and perfect."*

26

GENDER IDENTITY DISTORTION

"*So God created mankind in His own image, in the image of God He created them; male and female He created them.*" **Genesis 1:27**

From the beginning of creation, God made human beings beautifully, each one reflecting aspects of His divine image. This foundational truth, that God created us male and female brings clarity in a world where gender confusion and transgender identity struggles have become more common and culturally accepted, particularly among those carrying unresolved trauma.

Jesus said, "*The thief comes only to steal and kill and destroy; I have come that they may have life and have it to the full.*" **– John 10:10**. One of Satan's primary strategies is to attack our God-given identity through deception and spiritual identity theft, distorting, confusing, and ultimately attempting to destroy what God has declared "*very good*" **(Genesis 1:31)**.

For many who struggle with gender dysphoria, the roots often go deeper than internal or external feelings. These struggles can stem from past wounds or trauma, where confusion was sown through pain and abuse. In such cases, self-perception becomes distorted, and individuals may dissociate from their birth gender as a protective survival mechanism.

"*I praise you because I am fearfully and wonderfully made; your works are wonderful, I know that full well.*" **– Psalm 139:14**

Severe trauma can lead to dissociative responses, where parts of the self split from the core identity. A person may reject their biological gender because it feels too connected to a time of vulnerability, shame, or helplessness. In these cases, adopting an alternate gender identity can become an unconscious way to create emotional distance from pain, regain perceived control, and find a sense of safety.

"*The god of this age has blinded the minds of unbelievers so that they cannot see the light of the gospel that displays the glory of Christ, who is the image of God.*" **– 2 Corinthians 4:4**

While the world increasingly promotes gender-affirming care—social, medical, or surgical measures to align outward identity with internal feelings, this approach often bypasses deeper emotional, psychological, and spiritual roots, including trauma. Though it may offer temporary relief, it doesn't address the underlying wounds that shape a distorted identity.

Research consistently shows that individuals experiencing gender dysphoria or identifying as transgender face significantly higher rates of depression, anxiety, suicidal ideation, and self-harm than the general population. This underscores the need for compassionate, holistic care that acknowledges both the emotional and spiritual dimensions of identity.

The good news is this: healing is possible. Many individuals have found true restoration by confronting their painful past, receiving godly counsel, and embracing the identity given to them in Christ and by God. You, or those you love and support—can also find hope, freedom, and purpose by anchoring your identity in the truth of God's love and who you were created to be by the original Creator.

TESTIMONIES OF HEALING FROM GENDER CONFUSION

The following testimonies highlight the transforming power of Jesus and reveal common patterns behind gender identity struggles; many of which are rooted in childhood trauma, emotional wounds, or unmet needs and neglect.

Laura Perry lived nearly nine years as a transgender man before de-transitioning. In her book **Transgender to Transformed**, she shares how a personal encounter with Christ led her to embrace her God-given identity. She reveals that unresolved emotional pain and spiritual emptiness were at the core of her gender confusion.

Kathy Grace Duncan lived for eleven years as a man. After coming to Christ, she recognized how childhood trauma and unmet emotional needs influenced her identity struggles. Today, she serves as the Women's Ministry Leader at Portland Fellowship, helping others navigate similar paths toward healing.

David Arthur identified as transgender and lived as a woman for over twenty years. Through faith in Christ, he found healing from deep wounds and now leads I Belong, Amen! Ministries, guiding others to discover their true identity in Christ.

Walt Heyer lived as a transgender woman named Laura Jensen for eight years. Through therapy and a renewed relationship with God, he discovered that his gender dysphoria stemmed from early trauma, including cross-dressing encouraged by his grandmother and sexual abuse by an uncle. Now an author and speaker, he encourages others to explore the emotional and psychological roots of their struggles before pursuing irreversible changes. His books include **Trading My Sorrows** and **Paper Genders.**

God's design includes distinct and beautiful expressions of male and female that reflect His creative purpose: *"A woman must not wear men's clothing, nor a man wear women's clothing, for the Lord your God detests anyone who does this."* — **Deuteronomy 22:5**

Scripture also affirms that our bodies are sacred and should be honored as God created them: *"Do you not know that your bodies are temples of the Holy Spirit, who is in you, whom you have received from God? You are not your own; you were bought at a price. Therefore honor God with your bodies."* — **1 Corinthians 6:19–20**

True transformation comes not by changing outward appearances but through the renewal of the mind and heart: *"Therefore, if anyone is in Christ, the new creation has come: The old has gone, the new is here!"* — **2 Corinthians 5:17**

The enemy seeks to distort and destroy God's design for identity. But God's love is unchanging, and He promises healing to all who turn to Him: *"Draw near to God and He will draw near to you."* — **James 4:8** *"He has sent me to bind up the brokenhearted, to proclaim freedom for the captives and release from darkness for the prisoners."* — **Isaiah 61:1** *"He has sent me... to proclaim recovery of sight for the blind."* — **Luke 4:18**

This spiritual blindness refers to the lies of the enemy that obscure how we see ourselves and our Creator. Jesus brings light and clarity, restoring our vision to see who we truly are in Him: fearfully and wonderfully made.

GENDER IDENTITY REFLECTION

Our gender is a foundational aspect of the identity God has given us. This reflection and assessment are designed to help uncover potential sources of confusion and guide you toward healing and restoration in Christ. *"For you created my inmost being; you knit me together in my mother's womb."* — **Psalm 139:13**

Note: Some of these questions may bring up difficult emotions. It is wise to process them with a trusted Christian counselor, pastor, or supportive friend as you seek healing.

Prayerfully consider the following. Check any experiences that apply to you:

Early Life Experiences Assessment

- [ ] Experienced trauma/abuse that affected how you view yourself as male or female
- [ ] Felt rejected or shamed for expressing gender-appropriate behaviors
- [ ] Had a difficult or absent relationship with a parent that caused confusion
- [ ] Experienced identity confusion during early developmental years
- [ ] Received messages that your gender was disappointing or unwanted
- [ ] Was bullied for not fitting cultural or social gender stereotypes
- [ ] Felt unsafe or vulnerable in your own body
- [ ] Witnessed unhealthy or distorted relationship patterns between men and women
- [ ] Believed life would be better or easier if you were the opposite gender
- [ ] Experienced parental divorce that affected your understanding of gender roles
- [ ] Felt abandoned by a parent through death, divorce, or emotional distance
- [ ] Witnessed a parent being mistreated or abused

Reflection: Choose one or more of the experiences you checked. Briefly journal about the earliest memory associated with it. How did it make you feel? In what ways might it have shaped your understanding of your gender or identity?

_____

_____

_____

_____

"The Lord is close to the brokenhearted and saves those who are crushed in spirit."
— **Psalm 34:18**

Please see the spiritual warfare chapter for specific strategies to combat gender identity confusion.

Protective Mechanisms

When trauma occurs, the mind often develops protective responses to shield us from pain. These mechanisms, while initially helpful for survival, can sometimes contribute to confusion about identity—including gender identity. Reflect prayerfully and consider whether any of the following statements resonate with your experience:

- [ ] Believed that identifying as another gender would provide safety or protection
- [ ] Felt that being your biological gender made you vulnerable
- [ ] Created internal "parts" with different gender identities to cope with pain/memories
- [ ] Noticed that gender confusion intensified during or after stressful/traumatic events
- [ ] Experienced emotional distance from painful memories through gender dysphoria
- [ ] Believed that changing gender would resolve deep emotional issues
- [ ] Used thoughts of gender transition as an escape from unrelated struggles
- [ ] Experienced temporary relief from anxiety/depression by focusing on another gender
- [ ] Developed gender confusion as a response to sexual abuse or assault
- [ ] Felt more in control by adopting a different gender identity
- [ ] Found gender confusion to be a distraction from other life challenges
- [ ] Found comfort in believing your problems stemmed from being *"born in the wrong body"*
- [ ] Used gender identity as a way to gain acceptance in certain social groups
- [ ] Felt that a different gender identity would make you more lovable or acceptable
- [ ] Used gender dysphoria to create emotional distance from family members

Reflection Prompt: If you checked any of the boxes above, pause and ask yourself: What specific pain or wound might your mind be trying to protect you from? Invite the Holy Spirit to bring gentle clarity and healing to the roots of your struggle. *"He heals the brokenhearted and binds up their wounds."* — **Psalm 147:3**

_____

_____

_____

_____

Please see the spiritual warfare chapter for specific strategies to combat gender identity confusion.

Messages and Influences

Our understanding of gender is often shaped by the messages we receive—both spoken and unspoken from family, culture, media, and peers. These influences can deeply affect how we perceive ourselves and interpret our experiences.

Reflect and prayerfully consider whether any of the following apply to your journey:

- [ ] Absorbed cultural messages suggesting that gender is fluid or self-determined
- [ ] Received acceptance primarily when expressing traits of the opposite gender
- [ ] Found a sense of community in groups that encouraged non-traditional gender expression
- [ ] Noticed increased attention or care when expressing gender confusion
- [ ] Were told that happiness comes from aligning external appearance with internal feelings
- [ ] Received messaging that questioning your gender automatically means you should transition
- [ ] Had therapists affirm gender confusion without exploring underlying emotional or trauma-related causes
- [ ] Were influenced by social media suggesting gender choice is the path to fulfillment
- [ ] Knew others who transitioned and appeared happier afterward
- [ ] Received negative attention when expressing gender confusion
- [ ] Felt pressured to conform to rigid gender stereotypes that didn't reflect your personality
- [ ] Explored online communities that promoted gender fluidity
- [ ] Viewed gender change as a solution to social or relational difficulties
- [ ] Internalized the belief that discomfort with your body means you're transgender
- [ ] Believed that certain personality traits or interests meant you were "born in the wrong body"
- [ ] Received the message that gender identity confusion should always be affirmed but never questioned
- [ ] Were told that puberty blockers or hormone treatments are fully reversible and without long-term effects

Heart Check: How have these external influences shaped your beliefs about yourself? Which messages have had the strongest impact on how you see your gender and identity?

"See to it that no one takes you captive through hollow and deceptive philosophy, which depends on human tradition and the elemental spiritual forces of this world rather than on Christ." **— Colossians 2:8**

Please see the spiritual warfare chapter for specific strategies to combat gender identity confusion.

Spiritual Discernment: Reflecting on Gender Identity Through a Spiritual Lens

As you explore questions surrounding gender identity, it's important to consider the spiritual dimension. Scripture teaches that we are in a spiritual battle, and confusion about identity is often a key area where the enemy seeks to distort God's truth. Use this checklist to prayerfully evaluate your experiences.

Spiritual Reflection Assessment Check any that resonate with your experience:

- [ ] Feel disconnected from God when thinking about your gender identity
- [ ] Experience increased spiritual warfare when pursuing healing for gender-related confusion
- [ ] Notice that gender dysphoria intensifies during times of spiritual growth
- [ ] Feel resistance to Scriptures that affirm God's design for male and female
- [ ] Struggle to believe that you are "fearfully and wonderfully made" (Psalm 139:14)
- [ ] Experience shame or condemnation (rather than conviction) around gender-related issues
- [ ] Feel that God is distant or disapproving because of your gender struggles
- [ ] Sense spiritual opposition when seeking biblical counseling for gender identity
- [ ] Find it difficult to pray about gender-related questions
- [ ] Experience intrusive thoughts that contradict God's truth about your identity
- [ ] Notice increased spiritual attacks when considering embracing your biological gender
- [ ] Feel drawn away from Christian community when focusing on gender dysphoria
- [ ] Experience spiritual "heaviness" when pursuing transition or gender change
- [ ] Feel spiritually attacked when reading biblical perspectives on gender
- [ ] Sense internal conflict between your faith and your gender identity exploration
- [ ] Notice a pattern of withdrawing from God when gender confusion increases
- [ ] Feel tempted to reject parts of Scripture that affirm God's design for male and female
- [ ] Experience confusion or uncertainty in prayer about your gender identity

Prayer Pause: Take a moment to invite God into this reflection:

"Lord, show me where Your truth differs from the enemy's lies about my identity. Help me see myself through Your eyes." *"For God is not a God of confusion but of peace."*
— 1 Corinthians 14:33

_____

_____

_____

Please see the spiritual warfare chapter for specific strategies to combat gender identity confusion.

THE FALSE IDENTITY OF LABELS

Have you ever found yourself caught in the trap of labels? In today's culture, it's common for people to define themselves by descriptors—diagnoses, identities, affiliations, and characteristics they believe encapsulate who they are. While labels can offer clarity or validation in certain contexts, they become problematic when they replace our God-given identity.

At a recent healing conference, I observed a keynote speaker who introduced herself with a lengthy list of labels. She described herself as Doctor (Name), Puerto Rican, genderqueer, bilingual, mixed Spanish, African, Taino, chronically ill, neurodiverse, "a person of size," and "a system with DID." Despite speaking at a healing conference, her message offered little hope or encouragement. It was clear that she had become disconnected from a deeper sense of self—beyond the collection of labels she used to describe her experience. Rather than reflecting a grounded, whole identity, her self-description revealed fragmentation and unresolved pain.

When we define ourselves primarily through labels, several things can occur:

- We fragment our God-given identity into pieces
- We elevate certain characteristics above our core identity as image-bearers
- We prioritize temporary, earthly distinctions over eternal, spiritual realities
- We begin to see ourselves through the world's categories rather than God's eyes
- We limit our growth and healing by reinforcing fixed identities without hope of change
- We become confined within increasingly narrow definitions of self
- We foster division rather than unity—whether within the body of Christ or in the inherent connection we share as human beings made in God's image.
- We may use labels as shields to avoid true vulnerability
- We risk finding belonging in shared labels instead of shared faith
- We allow temporary conditions to define our permanent identity

The Biblical View of Identity

God's Word affirms that while we all have unique characteristics and life experiences, these do not define our core identity. God does not ignore our individuality, but He places it within the context of who we are in Him. Our primary identity is as sons and daughters of God—redeemed, restored, and made new in Christ.

"There is neither Jew nor Gentile, neither slave nor free, nor is there male and female, for you are all one in Christ Jesus." **— Galatians 3:28**

"Here there is no Gentile or Jew, circumcised or uncircumcised, barbarian, Scythian, slave or free, but Christ is all, and is in all." **— Colossians 3:11**

Let us choose to live from our true identity—not from labels imposed by others or adopted through pain, but from the truth of who we are in Christ.

COMMON LABELS THAT BECOME FALSE IDENTITIES

Check any labels you may have allowed to define you more than your identity in Christ:

- [ ] Medical or mental health diagnoses
- [ ] Career title or professional role
- [ ] Relationship status, personality type, or social media identity
- [ ] Sexuality or gender identity
- [ ] Cultural, socioeconomic, or ethnic background
- [ ] Political affiliation
- [ ] Educational level
- [ ] Past trauma or survivor status
- [ ] Physical appearance or body image
- [ ] Age or generational identity
- [ ] Religious role or church position
- [ ] Parenting status or family role

Reflection Question: How might any of these labels have overshadowed your primary identity as God's beloved child?

Use the following statements to help identify and release false agreements, break free of label identity, and receive the truth of who you are in God's eyes:

"I have believed that being _____ defines who I am."

"I renounce the lie that my identity is primarily defined by _____."

"I am a child of God, a co-heir with Christ, intentionally created by my loving Father."

Learn to reframe labels as part of your experience, not the definition of your identity.

For example: "While I experience _____, it is only one aspect of my life journey—not who I am at my core."

Replace identity statements with empowering language. Instead of saying, "I am bipolar," say, "I have bipolar disorder, but it does not define me."

Immerse yourself in Scripture that affirms your identity in Christ. Choose verses to memorize and recite daily to renew your mind with truth.

Begin prayer with identity-focused gratitude, such as, "Thank You, Father, that I am Your beloved child," rather than immediately focusing on struggles.

Surround yourself with people who see and affirm you as God does—those who speak life into your identity rather than reinforce limiting labels.

Heavenly Father, I repent for accepting labels as my primary identity. Forgive me for allowing the world's definitions to override the identity You've given me. I choose to find my identity as Your beloved child. Help me see myself as You see me, created with purpose, redeemed in love, and destined for eternity with You. In Jesus' name, Amen.

HOW FEAR AFFECTS OUR IDENTITY

Fear is a significant barrier to embracing our true identity in Christ. It creates what I call a "fear-driven, shaky identity"—one that fluctuates with external circumstances instead of being rooted in the unchanging truth of who God says we are. When fear takes root, it distorts and warps our perspective and causes us to see ourselves through a faulty lens rather than through God's eyes.

This distortion manifests in several key ways:

Isolation and Disconnection— Fear causes us to withdraw from community, preventing our true identity from being affirmed.

Performance-Based Identity— Fear leads us to base our worth on success, driven by the fear that we're not enough as we are.

Unstable Identity— A fear-driven identity is like a house built on sand, shifting with circumstances rather than being anchored in Christ.

Inhibited Purpose— Fear stops us from pursuing meaningful goals or discovering our true purpose.

The Theological Connection: Fear vs. Identity in Christ

Scripture teaches a clear connection between fear and identity. *"God has not given us a spirit of fear, but of power and of love and of a sound mind."* — **2 Timothy 1:7** Fear takes control when our identity is rooted in external things or the opinions of others, pulling us away from the truth of who we are in Christ.

How Fear-Driven Identity Manifests

- Fear of Abandonment: If you fear losing relationships, your identity will easily be shaken.
- Fear of Disappointment: If you fear disappointing others, you'll compromise your authenticity.
- Fear of Conflict: If you fear anger, you'll retreat from your true self to avoid conflict.
- Fear of Inadequacy: If you fear not being "good enough," you'll change your actions and sacrifice your true identity for approval.

Consider:

Which of these patterns do you recognize in your own life? How has fear shaped your identity? How can you root yourself in God's truth?

HOW FEAR AFFECTS OUR IDENTITY

Check which fears affect your sense of identity:

☐ Fear of rejection   ☐ Fear of failure

☐ Fear of abandonment   ☐ Fear of not being good enough

☐ Fear of disapproval   ☐ Fear of conflict

☐ Fear of vulnerability   ☐ Fear of criticism

☐ Fear of being seen for who I really am

☐ Fear of disappointing others

Note: Some fears in adulthood may stem from the wounded child within who still feels triggered in the present day. This is not your fault. Fears rooted in abusive or traumatic childhood experiences must be acknowledged in order to receive healing from Jesus. Through Him, new and healthier ways of coping can be learned.

The Truth That Sets Us Free

When we understand our true identity in Christ, fear begins to lose its power over us:

"You did not receive a spirit of slavery to fall back into fear, but you have received a spirit of adoption." —**Romans 8:15**

"Perfect love casts out fear." —**1 John 4:18**

Journal: What would change if you viewed yourself primarily through God's eyes rather than through the lens of your fears?

Later in this study, we will explore specific fears more deeply in the Fear Ladder exercise, (found on page 55) which will help you identify individual fears and the lies that fuel them. For now, simply recognize that fear may be keeping you from fully embracing your identity in Christ.

"Your purpose is often found *in what breaks your heart.*"

Bob Goff

DOODLE PAGE

What purposes has God whispered in your heart?

CHAPTER 4

Your Identity in Christ

JESUS KNEW HIS IDENTITY

"Then Jesus came from Galilee to John at the Jordan to be baptized by him. And John tried to prevent Him, saying, 'I need to be baptized by You, and are You coming to me?' But Jesus answered and said to him, 'Permit it to be so now, for thus it is fitting for us to fulfill all righteousness.' Then he allowed Him. When He had been baptized, Jesus came up immediately from the water; and behold, the heavens were opened to Him, and He saw the Spirit of God descending like a dove and alighting upon Him. And suddenly a voice came from heaven, saying, 'This is My beloved Son, in whom I am well pleased.'" — **Matthew 3:13–17 (NKJV)**

God the Father made a divine proclamation from heaven, through His Spirit, declaring Jesus as His beloved Son, in whom He was well pleased. The term beloved in Scripture means being completely, fully, and thoroughly loved. The word pleased conveys approval, satisfaction, and delight. This affirmation was a public declaration of Jesus' identity—righteous, faithful, and the fulfillment of God's will. Jesus knew that He was the Son of God. He knew God as His Father and was fully assured of being thoroughly and completely loved by Him. Jesus understood who He was. He and the Father were one, and He knew the Father intimately. *"My sheep hear My voice, and I know them, and they follow Me. I give them eternal life, and they will never perish, and no one will snatch them out of My hand. My Father, who has given them to Me, is greater than all, and no one is able to snatch them out of the Father's hand. I and the Father are one."* — **John 10:27–30** *In this passage, Jesus affirms both His divine identity and His relationship with God the Father. He speaks of the unity between them, revealing His divine nature and unshakable confidence in who He was.*

KEY MOMENTS IN JESUS' LIFE THAT REVEALED HIS IDENTITY:

1. Before His Birth – The angel Gabriel announced to Mary that she would give birth to "the Son of the Most High." **(Luke 1:26–38)**
2. As an Infant in the Temple – Simeon and Anna recognized Him as the promised Messiah. **(Luke 2:29–32)**
3. At Age Twelve – Jesus stayed behind in the temple, saying, "Did you not know that I must be in My Father's house?" **(Luke 2:49)**
4. During Temptation – Jesus resisted Satan's attempts to challenge His identity by standing firm on God's Word. **(Matthew 4:1–11)**
5. Throughout His Ministry – Jesus continually revealed His identity to His disciples, culminating in Peter's confession: "You are the Christ, the Son of the living God." **(Matthew 16:16–17)**

In what ways do you struggle to believe your identity as God's beloved child?

How might your life change if you were as secure in your identity as Jesus was?

OUR TRUE IDENTITY IN CHRIST

The following passage from Scripture provides a powerful foundation for understanding our true identity in Christ:

"Blessed be the God and Father of our Lord Jesus Christ, who has blessed us with every spiritual blessing in the heavenly places in Christ, just as He chose us in Him before the foundation of the world, that we should be holy and without blame before Him in love, having predestined us to adoption as sons by Jesus Christ to Himself, according to the good pleasure of His will, to the praise of the glory of His grace, by which He made us accepted in the Beloved. In Him we have redemption through His blood, the forgiveness of sins, according to the riches of His grace which He made to abound toward us in all wisdom and prudence, having made known to us the mystery of His will, according to His good pleasure which He purposed in Himself, that in the dispensation of the fullness of the times He might gather together in one all things in Christ, both which are in heaven and which are on earth—in Him. In Him also we have obtained an inheritance, being predestined according to the purpose of Him who works all things according to the counsel of His will, that we who first trusted in Christ should be to the praise of His glory. In Him you also trusted, after you heard the word of truth, the gospel of your salvation; in whom also, having believed, you were sealed with the Holy Spirit of promise, who is the guarantee of our inheritance until the redemption of the purchased possession, to the praise of His glory." **Ephesians 1:3-14**

When we accept Jesus' sacrifice, we are made new—new creations in Him. Our former identity rooted in the world is replaced with an unshakable identity as Daughters of the Most High God. This new identity in Christ cannot be taken from us, regardless of what we have done or what has been done to us.

Scripture Reflection:

Underline or highlight the phrases in **Ephesians 1** that begin with **"in Him"** or **"in Christ."**
Circle the words that describe what God has done for you.
From this passage, list 4 specific truths God says about who God says you are:

Personal Reflection:

Which aspect of your identity in Christ is most difficult for you to believe? Why?
How would your life be different if you fully embraced your identity as described in this passage?

For a complete list of Scripture verses on our identity in Christ, please refer to Appendix A: Going Deeper—Our Identity in Christ Scripture References starting on page 202.

◇**ACCEPTED**◇ EPHESIANS 1:6

◇**ADOPTED**◇ EPHESIANS 1:5, ROMANS 8:15

◇**AMBASSADORS FOR CHRIST**◇ 2 CORINTHIANS 5:20

◇**BELOVED**◇ EPHESIANS 1:6, SONG OF SOLOMON 6:3

◇**BRANCH OF THE TRUE VINE**◇ JOHN 15:5

◇**CALLED TO HIS KINGDOM AND GLORY**◇ 1 THESSALONIANS 2:12

◇**CHILDREN OF GOD**◇ JOHN 1:12, ROMANS 8:16, 1 JOHN 3:1

◇**CHOSEN**◇ EPHESIANS 1:4, COLOSSIANS 3:12

◇**CITIZENS OF HEAVEN**◇ PHILIPPIANS 3:20-21

◇**CO-HEIRS/JOINT-HEIRS WITH CHRIST**◇ ROMANS 8:17

◇**FEARFULLY AND WONDERFULLY MADE**◇ PSALM 139:14

◇**FORGIVEN**◇ EPHESIANS 1:7

◇**FRIEND OF GOD**◇ JOHN 15:15

◇**GOD'S TEMPLE**◇ 1 CORINTHIANS 3:16

◇**GOD'S WORKMANSHIP**◇ EPHESIANS 2:10

◇**HEIRS OF THE INHERITANCE**◇ EPHESIANS 1:11

◇**HIDDEN WITH CHRIST IN GOD**◇ COLOSSIANS 3:3

◇**HOLY AND BLAMELESS**◇ EPHESIANS 1:4, COLOSSIANS 3:12

◇**LIGHT OF THE WORLD**◇ MATTHEW 5:14

◇**MORE THAN CONQUERORS**◇ ROMANS 8:37

◇**NEW CREATIONS**◇ 2 CORINTHIANS 5:17

◇**OVERCOMERS**◇ 1 JOHN 5:4

◇**PARTAKERS OF THE DIVINE NATURE**◇ 2 PETER 1:4

◇**PREDESTINED**◇ EPHESIANS 1:5, EPHESIANS 1:11

◇**REDEEMED**◇ EPHESIANS 1:7

◇**ROYAL PRIESTHOOD**◇ 1 PETER 2:9

◇**SAINTS**◇ EPHESIANS 1:1

◇**SALT OF THE EARTH**◇ MATTHEW 5:13

◇**SAVED**◇ EPHESIANS 1:13

◇**SEALED WITH THE HOLY SPIRIT**◇ EPHESIANS 1:13

◇**SET APART**◇ 1 PETER 2:9

◇**VICTORIOUS**◇ 1 CORINTHIANS 15:57

JESUS' IDENTITY AND YOURS

Just as Jesus confidently lived from His identity as the Son of God, we are also called to live from the truth of who we are as God's beloved children. When we compare Jesus' identity with our own, we begin to see that our identity is secure—rooted in Christ and affirmed by God the Father.

Compare and Connect

JESUS' IDENTITY	YOUR IDENTITY
Beloved Son	Beloved child of God
Pleased the Father	Accepted in the Beloved
One with the Father	United with Christ
Knew His purpose	Created for purpose
Resisted temptation with truth	Can overcome through God's Word

When you know who you
are in Christ,
you can boldly proclaim your
identity in Him
clothing yourself with the endless
beauty of His grace,
the richness of His love
as you rest in the
truth about who you are.
~Sharri Burggraaf

LIVING FROM YOUR TRUE IDENTITY

Will you continue to live under the identity given to you by your earthly parents, past experiences, or the opinions of others—or will you embrace the identity God has given you? Accepting your true identity as a child of God is a choice of the will, an intentional decision to align your thoughts and heart with His truth. Transformation begins by renewing your mind, anchoring your identity on the unshakable foundation of Jesus Christ and the eternal reality of who you are in relationship with Him. Imagine your new identity as a fresh garment. Though the old garment may feel familiar and broken in, the new nature might feel uncomfortable at first. Over time, as you continue to walk in truth, it will begin to feel like your own.

Practical Steps:

- When getting dressed each morning, speak aloud the truths of God's Word to renew your mind and clothe yourself in your identity in Christ.
- Put on the promises of God and wrap yourselves in His truth
- Understand that embracing your new nature requires daily commitment.
- As you intentionally walk in your identity as a daughter of the Most High God, it may feel unfamiliar—but with perseverance, your heart will align with His truth.

Daily Declaration: I, _____, am a daughter of the Most High God who is _____, _____, and _____ in Christ.

My Identity Commitment: This week, I will remind myself of my true identity in Christ by:

☐ Speaking truth declarations each morning
☐ Writing an identity verse on my mirror
☐ Setting phone reminders with Scripture
☐ Sharing with a friend when I struggle

Boldly proclaim your identity in Christ as you clothe yourself with in the endless beauty of His grace, the richness of His love, and the rest found in knowing who you truly are.

Write your own affirmations in a journal to remind yourself daily of who God says you are or in the back of the book on page 200.

When you fully realize your identity in Christ, your purpose will become more evident, and fear will have no power over you.

~Michelle McClain-Watters~

In Christ

ADOPTED   ACCEPTED   AMBASSADOR   ALIVE   ANOINTED
APPOINTED   ASSURED   BELONG   BELOVED   BLESSED
BLAMELESS   BOLD   BORN OF GOD   BOUGHT   BRANCH
BRAVE   BROUGHT NEAR   BUILT UP   CHILD OF GOD
CHOSEN   CITIZEN OF HEAVEN   CO-HEIR   CO-WORKER
COMPLETE   CONFIDENT   CONQUEROR   COURAGEOUS
DARK TO LIGHT   DEAD TO SIN   DEBT PAID   DELIGHTED IN
DELIVERED   DIRECT ACCESS TO GOD   DISCIPLE   EMPOWERED
ELEVATED   ESTABLISHED   EXONERATED   FIRMLY ROOTED
FORGIVEN   FRAGRANCE OF CHRIST   FREE   FRIEND
GOD'S WORKMANSHIP   HEIR OF GOD   HEALED
HELPED BY GOD   HIDDEN WITH CHRIST   HOLY
HAVE HOPE   INDWELT   INNOCENT   INTERCEEDED FOR
JUSTIFIED   JESUS' FRIEND   KNOWN   KINGS' CHILD
KEPT   LIGHT   LOVED   LIVING STONE   MEMBER OF CHRIST
MIND OF CHRIST   MINISTER OF RECONCILIATION
NEEDS ARE MET   NEW CREATION   NEW CREATURE
NOT ALONE   NOT CONDEMNED   NOT HELPLESS
ONE WITH HIM   OVERCOMER   PEACE WITH GOD
PERFECTED   PERSONAL WITNESS   PREDESTINED   PRINCE
PRINCESS   PROMISED BY GOD   PROTECTED   PURIFIED
QUICKENED TOGETHER WITH CHRIST   RECONCILED
REDEEMED   RESCUED FROM DARKNESS   RIGHTEOUS
SAINT   SAFE   SALT   SANCTIFIED   SAVED   SEALED
SEATED IN THE HEAVENLIES   SECURE   TEMPLE OF GOD
TO HIS PRAISE   TRANSFERRED INTO THE KINGDOM
TREASURED   UNITED WITH CHRIST   UNTO HIS GLORY
VICTORIOUS   VALUED   WANTED   WASHED   WORTHY
X-AMPLE   X-EMPT   X-CRUCIFIED   YOKED TOGETHER
WITH OTHER BELIEVERS   ZEALOUS FOR CHRIST

"See, I have engraved you on the palms of my hands..." Isaiah 49:16

FINGERPRINT OF GOD

We've explored the foundational truths of our identity in Christ. In a world where every person possesses a unique fingerprint and a distinct DNA—one that sets them apart from all others—one profound truth remains: every human being is a miracle, intricately formed by the Creator and uniquely crafted in His image.

Just as fingerprints are used to identify a person, when someone accepts Christ, they are given a new spiritual identity. It is as though the very fingerprint of God is pressed upon their life, marking them as His own child. They are now identified as a daughter of the King—a citizen of heaven, belonging to the family of God.

"*See, I have engraved you on the palms of my hands...*" **Isaiah 49:16**

Once adopted into God's family, believers begin to reflect Christ. Just as children bear resemblance to their parents, we begin to display His character, nature, and love.

"*For those God foreknew He also predestined to be conformed to the image of His Son.*" — **Romans 8:29**

Imagine a forensic team dusting for fingerprints—not to convict, but to reveal who's been present. At the moment of your salvation, if heaven's forensic team were to dust the scene, they would find divine fingerprints—evidence that Jesus was there, that grace intervened, and that your guilt was placed on Him. "*In Him we have redemption through His blood, the forgiveness of sins, in accordance with the riches of God's grace.*" —**Ephesians 1:7**

Personal Reflection: Describe a time when you felt God's fingerprint on your life—a moment when you sensed His specific touch on your circumstances:

There is a divine fingerprint of God upon every believer. It is an eternal mark of ownership and love—an identification that you belong to Him, chosen, redeemed, and sealed by His Spirit as a co-heir of Christ. "*Now it is God who makes both us and you stand firm in Christ. He anointed us, set His seal of ownership on us, and put His Spirit in our hearts as a deposit, guaranteeing what is to come.*" —**2 Corinthians 1:21–22**

In the spiritual courtroom, Satan—"*the accuser of the brethren*"—acts as a prosecuting attorney, bringing charges based on past sins. He tries to gather evidence to condemn us, pointing to guilt, shame, and failure. But the fingerprints left behind at the scene of your past are no longer yours—they are covered by the prints of the Savior who took your place.

"*For the accuser of our brothers and sisters has been thrown down, who accuses them day and night before our God. But they have conquered him by the blood of the Lamb and by the word of their testimony.*" —**Revelation 12:10–11**

Though the enemy tries to control through lies, fear, and condemnation, God's fingerprint reminds us that we are no longer defined by our past. Our identity is sealed in Christ, and His touch remains on every chapter of our redeemed story.

Even though Satan seeks to "dust for fingerprints" in an attempt to find you guilty of your sins, you are declared innocent. Your Kinsman Redeemer paid the full ransom with His own life. Your Savior has released you from the prison of sin. Your Divine Defense Attorney stands before the Judge and proclaims you not guilty, overriding the accusations of the evil jury. Your Heavenly Bondsman has already paid your bail in full. *"And you also were included in Christ when you heard the message of truth, the gospel of your salvation. When you believed, you were marked in him with a seal, the promised Holy Spirit, who is a deposit guaranteeing our inheritance until the redemption of those who are God's possession—to the praise of his glory."* **Ephesians 1:13-14**

Divine Roles of Christ in Your Redemption

Which of these roles of Christ speaks to your heart today?

☐ **Kinsman Redeemer** - He paid the price to make you His own.

☐ **Savior** - He broke the chains and opened the prison doors of sin.

☐ **Defense Attorney** - He pleads your case and declares you innocent.

☐ **Bondsman** - He paid your debt completely.

☐ **King** - He adopted you into royalty and calls you His daughter.

☐ **Heir of All Things** - As the Firstborn, Jesus shares His divine inheritance, making you a co-heir with Him of eternal life, God's kingdom, all spiritual blessings, and your identity as His beloved daughter.

When we accept Christ, we receive a new and unique identity in Him. It's as if God presses His eternal fingerprint upon our lives, marking us as His very own. From that moment on, we no longer carry just our human identity—we carry the reflection of Christ. Though each of us possesses unique gifts, stories, and personalities, the divine character of Christ begins to be formed within us. Our garments of sin are exchanged for robes of righteousness, as declared in **Isaiah 61:10**, and we are crowned with honor, signifying our adoption as daughters of the King. As children of God, we are granted full rights of sonship and become co-heirs with Christ, sharing in the inheritance of the Father **(Romans 8:17; Galatians 4:7)**. We now bear His name, carry His image, and reflect His love. The divine fingerprint of God marks our lives with identity, purpose, and belonging.

Evidence of God's Fingerprints: Which signs of His transforming touch have you seen in your life?

- New desires to know God
- Changed priorities
- Different responses to difficulties
- Increased compassion for others
- Sensitivity to sin
- Love for God's Word

You are not who you once were. You belong to the One who paid the highest price for you, sealed you with His Spirit, and left His fingerprint on your soul; forever.

THE ENEMY'S ACCUSATIONS VS. GOD'S TRUTH

THE ENEMY SAYS...	BUT GOD SAYS...
"You've messed up too many times."	"You are forgiven and made new." 2 Corinthains 5:17
"You'll never be good enough."	"You are complete in Christ." Colossians 2:10
"You're defined by your past."	"You are a new creation." 2 Corinthians 5:17
"No one truly loves you."	"I have loved you with an everlasting love." Jeremiah 31:3
"You're all alone."	"I will never leave you nor forsake you." Hebrews 13:5

What "accusation fingerprints" has the enemy tried to use against you?

_____

_____

YOU are loved

CHAPTER 5

Identifying Your Fears

FEAR LADDER

EXERCISE
IDENTIFYING FEARS THAT IMPACT YOUR IDENTITY

Purpose of the Exercise: The Fear Ladder is a tool designed to help you recognize specific fears that may be shaping your sense of identity. By naming and examining these fears, you can begin the process of replacing them with God's truth about who you are in Christ.

Instructions:

Pray First: Begin with prayer, asking God to reveal any hidden fears that have influenced how you view yourself. Invite the Holy Spirit to bring clarity and insight.

List Your Fears: On the next page, write down all the fears that come to mind using the space provided in the bottom left corner. Don't worry about the order—just allow the fears to surface and write them freely.

Be Specific: Instead of listing general fears like "fear of rejection," try to be more precise. Clarity brings greater healing. For example:

"Fear of being rejected by my friends if they knew the real me"

"Fear of being rejected by my husband if I share my true feelings"

Arrange Your Fears: After listing your fears, identify which one has causes the most anxiety and has the strongest impact on your identity. Write that fear at the top rung of the ladder. Then arrange the others on subsequent rungs according to how deeply they affect you.

Reflect: As you place each fear, reflect on the ways it has influenced your:

– Self-perception

– Decision-making

– Interactions with others

– Relationship with God

Remember: The goal is not to dwell on fear but to bring it into the light of God's presence. Healing begins with truth and acknowledgment.

As **Psalm 34:4** declares, *"I sought the LORD, and He answered me; He delivered me from all my fears."*

FEAR LADDER

Now it's time to identify the specific fears that may be influencing your life and sense of identity. In the space provided at the bottom left, list any fears that come to mind—in no particular order. Then, place the most significant fear at the top rung of the ladder and arrange the remaining fears in descending order based on how deeply they affect you.

_____	1
_____	2
_____	3
_____	4
_____	5
_____	6
_____	7
_____	8
_____	9
_____	10
_____	11
_____	12
_____	13

NOTICE WHETHER THE OTHER FEARS ARE CONNECTED TO—OR STEM FROM—YOUR PRIMARY FEAR.

Take time to process any emotions that may surface during this exercise. Allow God to meet you in this space with compassion and truth.

"When we surrender our dreams to God, *He gives them back with purpose.*"

Levi Lusko

CHAPTER 6

Identifying The Lies You Believe

Identifying Lies

Beneath every fear identified in the previous section lies a deeper belief; a lie about ourselves, others, or God—that influences our behaviors, actions and identity. Begin this step in prayer, asking the Holy Spirit to reveal any lies, whether conscious or subconscious, that you may have come into agreement with.

We have a very real enemy—*the father of lies*—who often uses wounds from our past to deceive us. Satan's goal is to keep us bound in fear, to limit our effectiveness in the Kingdom of God. Fear can paralyze us, keeping us from fully living out the purpose God has for us. A life dominated by fear is a life not fully lived. But as **John 10:10** reminds us, Jesus came that "*we may have life, and have it abundantly*".

This exercise takes courage and radical honesty. Set aside a quiet, distraction-free space. The enemy does not want these lies exposed, because once brought into His light, they begin to lose their power. Expect some internal resistance—that's often a sign you're moving in the right direction toward freedom.

God does not condemn you for believing lies. His heart is to set you free from them. Throughout this process, be gentle with yourself. The Holy Spirit will guide you with compassion, revealing only what you're ready to face with His help.

Recognizing the lies you've believed is a critical step in your healing journey. Each lie identified is like removing a stone from the wall that's kept you from fully embracing your identity in Christ. Some lies may have originated in childhood—spoken by others or formed through painful experiences. Others may have taken root over the years through disappointments or personal struggles. No matter their source, these lies only hold power if you continue to believe them. As Jesus said in **John 8:32**, "*You will know the truth, and the truth will set you free.*"

As you reflect on each fear you listed, ask: *What am I really believing about myself in this area? What am I believing about God? What am I believing about others*? This honest questioning can uncover the root lies that have been shaping your thoughts, decisions, and self-perception. Identifying the lies we belives is not about shame or failure—it's about awareness and inviting God's truth to replace deception.

Example of Identifying a Lie: If you fear not being pretty or thin enough to be accepted, the underlying lie might be: "*I'm unlovable just the way that I am. I need to change my appearance to be loved.*"

For every fear on your list, identify the lies that you believe. On the next page, you'll find the 20 most common lies women believe. Review these, then list your personal lies on the page that follows.

COMMON LIES WOMEN BELIEVE

I am bad

I am worthless

I am unlovable

I am unwanted

God won't protect me

I am alone

I will never heal

I'm beyond forgiveness or redemption

I am a failure

I will always be afraid

I have no purpose

I am a mistake

No one cares about me

I cannot trust anyone

I will never be happy

I am ugly

I am weak

My past defines me

I am not enough

I am a burden

I am invisible/insignificant

I will never be able to forgive

God is angry with me

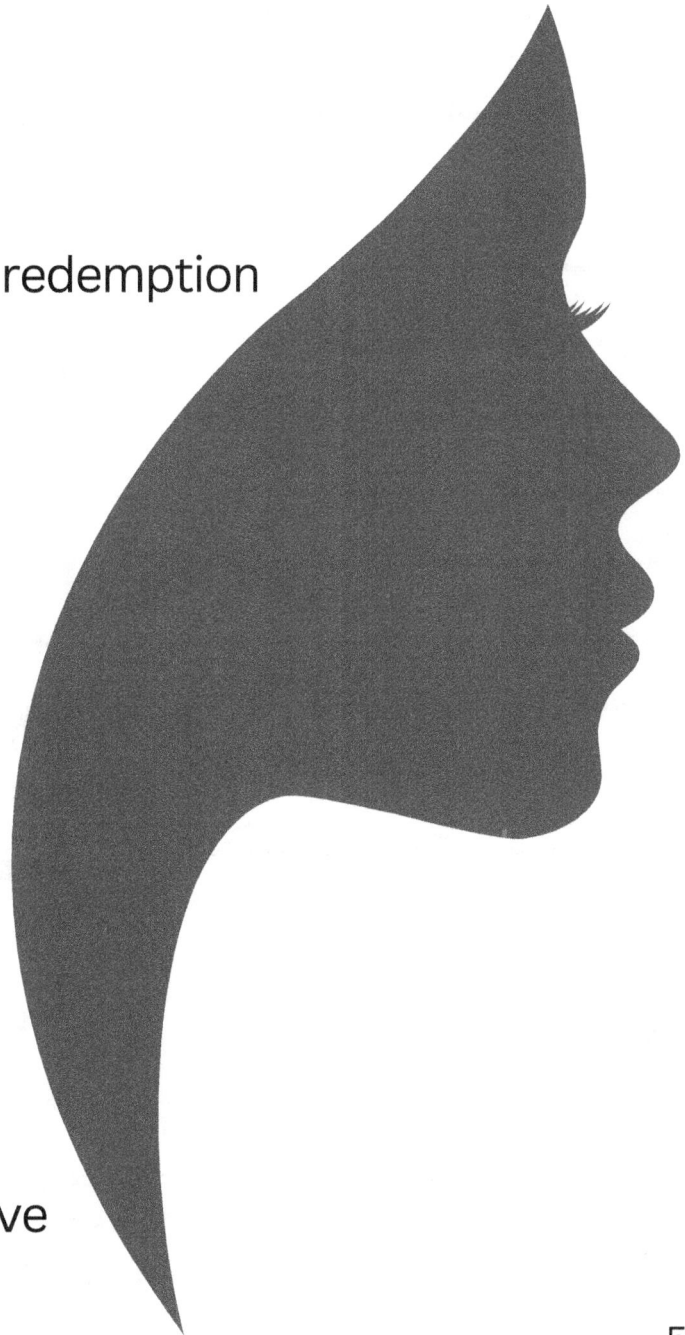

LIE LADDER

MAKE A LIST OF LIES YOU IDENTIFY

In the space on the bottom left, list the lies you identify in no specific order.
After you have listed them you will take the next step.

LIST YOUR TOP LIE ON THE TOP RUNG OF THE LADDER

List your other lies in the order of how impactful they are to you.

————————— 1

————————— 2

————————— 3

————————— 4

————————— 5

————————— 6

————————— 7

————————— 8

————————— 9

————————— 10

————————— 11

————————— 12

————————— 13

NOTICE WHETHER ANY OF THE OTHER LIES ARE CONNECTED TO—OR STEM FROM—THE ONE THAT IS IMPACTING YOU THE MOST.

Take time to process any emotions that may arise as a result of engaging in these exercises. You may wish to do this with a therapist, support person or friend.

RENOUNCING THE LIES

Now that you have identified the lies you've believed, it's time to call them what they are —lies. Breaking free from long-held falsehoods requires more than mere recognition. Scripture reveals that lying spirits seek to bind us through our agreement with deception. Whether knowingly or unknowingly, when we come into agreement with a lie, we give it influence over our thoughts, identity, and actions. This is why a formal renunciation is such a powerful step—it is a clear declaration that you no longer consent to the enemy's deception.

In **John 8:44**, Jesus describes Satan as *"a liar and the father of lies."* His strategy from the beginning has been to distort our understanding of God, ourselves, and others through falsehood. But we are not powerless. **Proverbs 18:21** reminds us, *"The tongue has the power of life and death."* When we verbally renounce lies, we are actively using our God-given authority to reject death-producing deception and choose to speak life-giving truth. This act of renunciation is also deeply biblical. Throughout Scripture, verbal declarations of truth are connected to spiritual freedom and covenant. In **Joshua 24:15**, Joshua declares, *"As for me and my household, we will serve the Lord."* **Romans 10:10** affirms, *"It is with your mouth that you profess your faith and are saved."* Speaking truth is not just symbolic—it is transformative.

As you prepare to renounce each lie, create a quiet, sacred space for this important spiritual work. Take your time. Allow the Holy Spirit to guide you through each one. You may experience strong emotions as these lies are confronted—this is natural, as many have been rooted deeply within your identity. With your list of lies in front of you, you are now ready to break agreement with them.

For each lie, pray this simple renunciation prayer:

"Father God, I come to You in the name of Jesus to renounce the lie that _____. I declare that this lie has no power over me, and I refuse to agree with it any longer. Thank You, Lord, for Your truth that sets me free. In Jesus' name, Amen."

By choosing to confront the lies that held you captive, you are already becoming the woman of purpose God intented you to be. Each lie you renounce is a chain that falls away, each truth you declare is a step deeper into freedom. The enemy's greatest fear is a woman who knows her identity in Christ—because such a woman is unstoppable. Today, you choose identity over insecurity, inheritance over the enemy's intimidation, and truth over deception. Your breakthrough is not coming—it is here. Exposing the lies are the first step. The next is to surrender both your fears and false beliefs to God, creating space for His truth to take root in your heart.

As you turn the page you'll find biblical truths to replace the 20 most common lies women believe. Review them carefully. Remember, declaring truth is the path to freedom.

LETTING GO AND SURRENDERING

The process of transformation—and embracing your identity in Christ—requires a willingness to surrender both the fears you've identified and the lies you've believed. When we experience trauma, we may unconsciously cling to these fears and falsehoods, believing they protect us where we may have felt God didn't. This creates a distorted view of both ourselves, God and others, leaving us with an unstable, insecure identity rather than one firmly rooted in Christ.

When we seek our identity in what we do, in the fears that grip our hearts, or in the lies we've internalized, we hold tightly to things that are both temporary and untrue. Picture your hands clenched around these fears and beliefs. While your hands remain closed, they form a barrier—shutting out God's gentle whispers of truth, the support of others, and the fullness of the life He intends for you.

Surrender is a courageous act of trust. It is never forced or demanded by God. Rather, it is a personal, voluntary choice to release what has kept you bound. True surrender flows from a place of love and faith—not obligation or pressure.

Now imagine opening your hands, palms facing upward, as you release each fear and lie you've identified. In this posture of surrender, you make room to receive God's abundant grace and truth. With open hands, you are ready to embrace your true identity—as a beloved daughter of the King, fearfully and wonderfully made. This sacred act of letting go prepares you for the next step: replacing lies with truth and stepping fully into the freedom Christ offers.

Open hands symbolize surrender. They are a sign of readiness to receive all that God longs to give you.

Prayer of Surrender:

Heavenly Father, In this moment of surrender, I lay before You all my striving for success, the fears that have driven me, and the lies I have believed. I release them into Your loving hands, trusting in Your promise to transform me and reveal my true identity in Christ. As I let go of these burdens, I open my heart to receive Your grace and truth. Help me embrace my identity as a beloved daughter of the King of Kings and Lord of Lords. May Your Holy Spirit guide me on this journey of renewal. Fill me with the assurance of Your unconditional love and acceptance. In Jesus' name, Amen.

CHAPTER 7

Identifying Truths from God's Word

TRUTHS FROM GOD'S WORD

I'm Inherently Good
I Have Much Worth
I'm Unconditionally Loved
I'm Wanted & Chosen
God Will Protect Me
I'm Never Alone
God Promises Healing
I'm Forgiven and Redeemed
I'm an Overcomer
I'm Courageous
I Have Purpose
I was Planned
God Cares For Me
I Can Trust God
I Can Find Joy & Happiness
I Am Beautiful
I Am Strong With God
My Past is Gone
I'm More Than Enough
I'm Not a Burden
I'm Seen & Significant
I Can Forgive With God's Grace
God is Not Angry

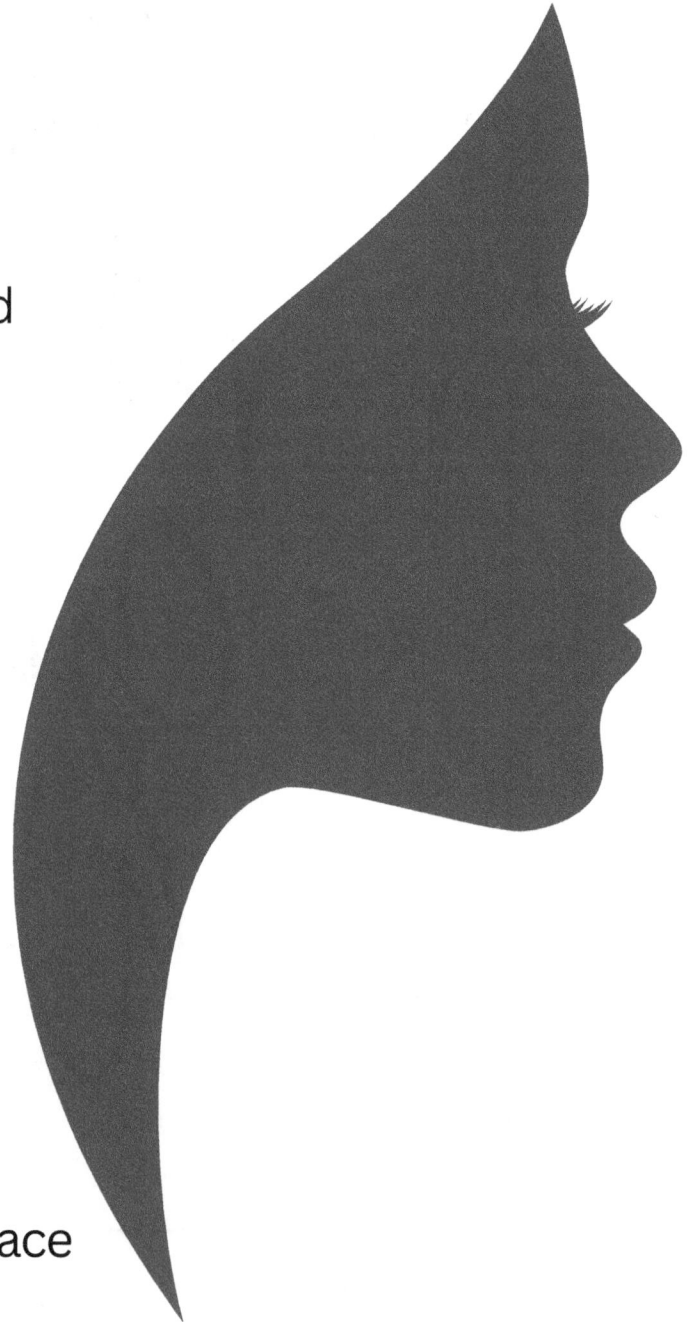

TRUTHS FROM GOD'S WORD

I'M INHERENTLY GOOD

"For we are God's handiwork, created in Christ Jesus to do good works, which God prepared in advance for us to do." **Ephesians 2:10**

I HAVE MUCH WORTH

"You are precious in my eyes, honored, and I love you." **Isaiah 43:4**

I'M UNCONDITIONALLY LOVED

"Neither height nor depth, nor anything else in all creation, is able to separate us from the love of God in Christ Jesus our Lord." **Romans 8:39**

I'M WANTED & CHOSEN

"You did not choose me, but I chose you and appointed you so that you might go and bear fruit—fruit that will last." **John 15:16**

GOD WILL PROTECT ME

"The Lord is my rock, my fortress and deliverer; my God is my rock, in whom I take refuge, my shield and horn of my salvation, my stronghold." **Psalm 18:2**

I'M NEVER ALONE

"I will never leave you nor forsake you." **Hebrews 13:5**

GOD PROMISES HEALING

"He heals the brokenhearted and binds up their wounds." **Psalm 147:3**

I'M FORGIVEN AND REDEEMED

"In Him we have redemption through his blood, the forgiveness of sins, in accordance with the riches of God's grace." **Ephesians 1:7**

I'M AN OVERCOMER

"I can do all things through Christ who strengthens me." **Philippians 4:13**

I'M COURAGEOUS

"For God has not given us a spirit of fear, but of power, love and a sound mind." **2 Timothy 1:7**

I HAVE PURPOSE

"For I know the plans I have for you," declares the LORD, "plans to prosper you and not to harm you, plans to give you hope and a future." **Jeremiah 29:11**

I WAS PLANNED

"Before I formed you in the womb I knew you, before you were born I set you apart." **Jeremiah 1:5**

GOD CARES FOR ME

"Cast all your anxiety on him because he cares for you." **1 Peter 5:7**

I CAN TRUST GOD

"Trust in the LORD with all your heart and lean not on your own understanding." **Proverbs 3:5**

I CAN FIND JOY & HAPPINESS

"The joy of the LORD is your strength." **Nehemiah 8:10**

I AM BEAUTIFUL

"You are altogether beautiful, my darling; there is no flaw in you." **Song of Songs 4:7**

I AM STRONG WITH GOD

"But those who hope in the LORD will renew their strength. They will soar on wings like eagles; they will run and not grow weary, they will walk and not be faint." **Isaiah 40:31**

MY PAST IS GONE

"Therefore, if anyone is in Christ, the new creation has come: The old has gone, the new is here!" **2 Corinthians 5:17**

I'M MORE THAN ENOUGH

"And God is able to bless you abundantly, so that in all things at all times, having all that you need, you will abound in every good work." **2 Corinthians 9:8**

I'M NOT A BURDEN

"Come to me, all you who are weary and burdened, and I will give you rest." **Matthew 11:28**

I'M SEEN & SIGNIFICANT

"Even the very hairs of your head are all numbered." **Matthew 10:30**

I CAN FORGIVE WITH GOD'S GRACE

"Be kind and compassionate to one another, forgiving each other, just as in Christ God forgave you." **Ephesians 4:32**

GOD IS NOT ANGRY

"The LORD is compassionate and gracious, slow to anger, abounding in love." **Psalm 103:8**

MORE TRUTHS FROM GOD'S WORD
ACCESSING THE APPENDIX
BIBLICAL TRUTHS TO COUNTER COMMON LIES

For deeper study and ongoing renewal of your mind, turn to Appendix B: Biblical Truths to Counter Common Lies, beginning on page 200. This section contains 20 dedicated pages—each focused on one of the most common lies women believe. Every page offers a collection of carefully selected Bible verses that directly address and refute that specific lie. These Scriptures are designed to strengthen your foundation in truth, helping you walk in freedom and embrace your identity in Christ.

Let God's Word be the loudest voice you hear.

YOUR PERSONAL TRUTH ARSENAL

Finding Your Personal Truths From God's Word

For every lie you have identified and renounced, it's essential to replace it with the unshakable truth of God's Word. Scripture is your ultimate source of truth—what God says about you is what you can confidently believe about yourself.

Use the section below to write your own personalized list of biblical truths:

- Choose Bible verses that directly refute the specific lies you once believed. (Refer to the appendix beginning on page 200)
- Insert your name into each verse to make it personal and impactful.
- Write the verses in present tense as declarations of truth.
- Focus on verses that speak directly to the heart of each lie you've renounced.

These personalized truths become your spiritual arsenal—powerful tools to silence the enemy's voice. Speak God's truths from His Word aloud daily. It is like God Himself is speaking over your life. Over time, these truths will take root, moving from head knowledge to heart belief, transforming the way you see yourself, the way you see God, and others. **Use this space to write your personal biblical truths:**

_____

_____

_____

_____

_____

_____

_____

_____

"We find our purpose when we stop asking "Who am I?" *and start asking "Whose am I?"*

Jennie Allen

CHAPTER 8

Speaking Truth

The Road to Freedom

SPEAKING YOUR TRUTH

Now that you are armed with the truth, begin the journey of renewing your mind.
Transformation doesn't happen overnight. Lasting change comes through the persistent declaration of God's truth which is your path to freedom.

- **Daily Declaration:** Speak your truth-filled verses aloud every day
- **Take Thoughts Captive:** When lies try to creep back in, immediately counter them with truth (**2 Corinthians 10:5**)
- **Persevere:** Mind renewal is a process, not a one-time event - **Romans 12:2** reminds us to "*be transformed by the renewing of your mind.*"
- **Celebrate Progress:** Pay attention to how your perspective begins to shift as truth takes root and grows within you.

Your identity is like your spiritual DNA—it comes from the eternal truth that you are created in the image of God. When you accept Jesus, He defines who you are and whose you are. As you continue this journey, your heart and mind will align with God's truth.

Truth Declaration Practice

In the space below, write a powerful truth statement that directly counters the most significant lie you've believed. Make it personal and present tense:

"I am _____."

Check the situations where you most need to remember and declare this truth:

- [ ] When I'm alone
- [ ] In social settings
- [ ] With family
- [ ] At work
- [ ] When I feel criticized
- [ ] When I face challenges
- [ ] In the morning
- [ ] Before bed
- [ ] Other: _____

I commit to speaking this declaration aloud ____ times each day for the next week.

Prayer for Truth

Lord, I choose to believe what You say about me rather than the lies I've believed. Help me to consistently renew my mind with Your Word until Your truth penetrates my heart and becomes more real to me than any lie. Transform my thoughts to align with Yours. When doubt creeps in, remind me of Your unchanging promises. In Jesus' name, Amen.

On the following page, you'll find "Biblical Declarations"—powerful "I am" statements you can speak over yourself daily to further reinforce God's truth about your identity.

BIBLICAL DECLARATIONS

USE THESE "I AM" STATEMENTS (WITH BIBLE VERSES)

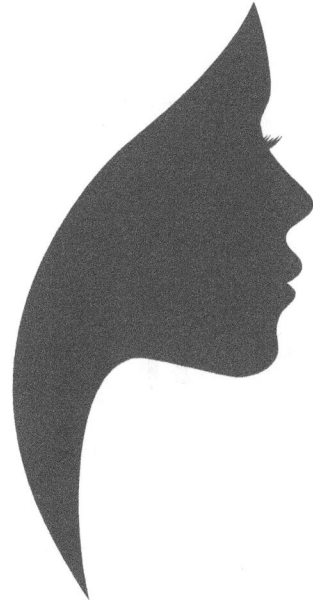

I am made new in Christ (2 Corinthians 5:17)

I am God's masterpiece (Ephesians 2:10)

I am deeply loved by God (Romans 5:8)

I am chosen by God (1 Peter 2:9)

God is my refuge and strength (Psalm 46:1)

God is always with me (Hebrews 13:5)

By His wounds, I am healed (Isaiah 53)

I am forgiven and redeemed (Ephesians 1:7)

I am more than a conqueror (Romans 8:37)

God has not given me a spirit of fear (2 Timothy 1:7)

I am called according to His purpose (Romans 8:28)

I am fearfully and wonderfully made (Psalm 139:14)

God cares for me (1 Peter 5:7)

I trust in the Lord with all my heart (Proverbs 3:5)

In His presence is fullness of joy (Psalm 16:11)

I am beautiful in God's sight (Song of Solomon 4:7)

I can do all things through Christ (Philippians 4:13)

I am a new creation in Christ (2 Corinthians 5:17)

God's grace is sufficient for me (2 Corinthians 12:9)

I am God's delight (Zephaniah 3:17)

I am seen and known by God (Psalm 139:1-2)

I can forgive through Christ (Ephesians 4:32)

God is gracious and compassionate (Psalm 103:8

"Our highest calling is not to do but to be –to be with Him."
Jackie Hill Perry

CHAPTER 9

Knowing God's Love

EMBRACING GOD'S LOVE

Before you can fully embrace your purpose, you must first understand how deeply loved and treasured you are by the God who created you. You are not a mistake. God created you intentionally, loves you unconditionally, and desires you as His own. His love for you is boundless—personal, intimate, active, and purposeful. He already knows everything about you, and His desire is that you would come to know Him deeply through a relationship with Him through Jesus Christ.

You were a planned creation for a purpose!
Underline or highlight the words that stand out to you.

PSALM 139:13-14

Fearfully and Wonderfully Made

'For you formed my inward parts; you knitted me together in my mother's womb. I praise you, for I am fearfully and wonderfully made. Wonderful are your works; my soul knows it very well.'

_____

_____

_____

_____

_____

_____

_____

_____

_____

Reflection: Spend a few minutes meditating on this verse. Write down how it causes you to feel to know you are "fearfully and wonderfully made."

Action Step: Create a personal affirmation using this verse and say it to yourself daily.

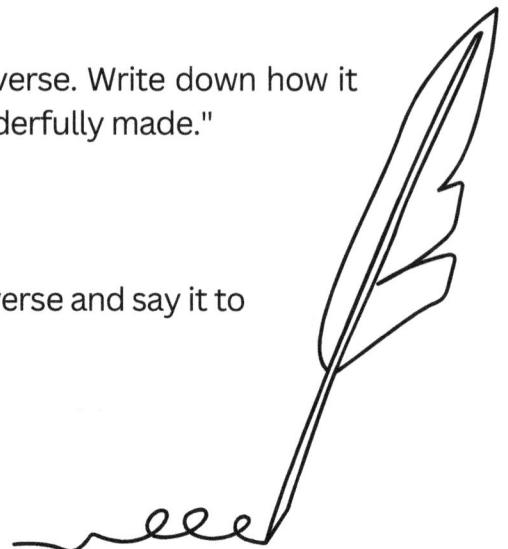

This foundational truth underscores the inherent value and dignity of every person and where we came from. Underline or highlight the words that stand out to you.

GENESIS 1:27

God created man in His image

"So God created man in His own image, in the image of God He created him; male and female He created them."

_____
_____
_____
_____
_____
_____
_____
_____

Reflection: Journal about what it means to you to be created in the image of God.

Action Step: Look in the mirror each day and remind yourself, "I am created in the image of God."

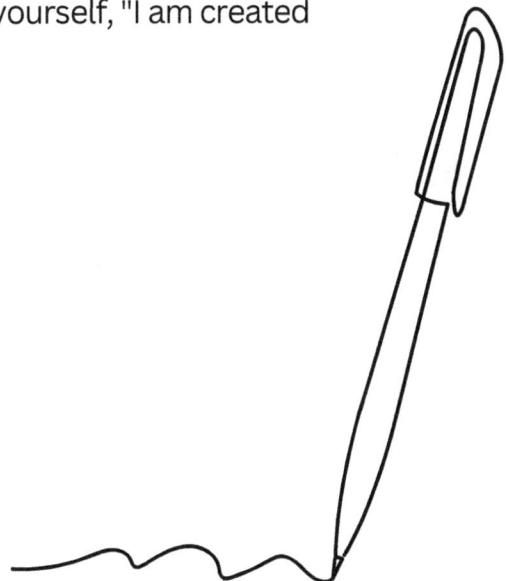

God's thoughts toward you are as countless as the grains of sand on the seashore. He loves you deeply and is fully invested in your well-being. As a Good Father, He surrounds you with grace, favor, and love. Through Jesus Christ, you have been given His righteousness. You are His masterpiece—cherished, chosen, and deeply beloved. Underline or highlight any words that stand out to you.

1 JOHN 4:16

God is love!

So we have come to know and to believe the love that God has for us. God is love, and whoever abides in love abides in God, and God abides in him.

Reflection: Journal about times when you have felt God's love in your life.

Action Step: Make a list of ways you can show God's love to others this week.

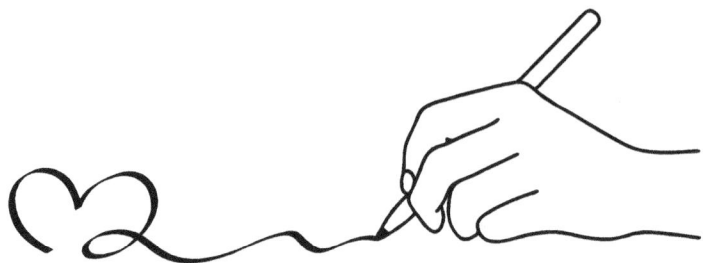

Embracing God's love and reflecting it to others is what we were created for. We were made for good works, which He prepared in advance for us to walk in—works rooted in His love. Underline or highlight any words that stand out to you.

EPHESIANS 2:10

Created for good works.

"For we are His workmanship, created in Christ Jesus for good works, which God prepared beforehand, that we should walk in them."

_____
_____
_____
_____
_____
_____
_____
_____
_____

Reflection: Journal about the good works you feel God has prepared for you.

Action Step: Plan a specific act of kindness or service you can do this week.

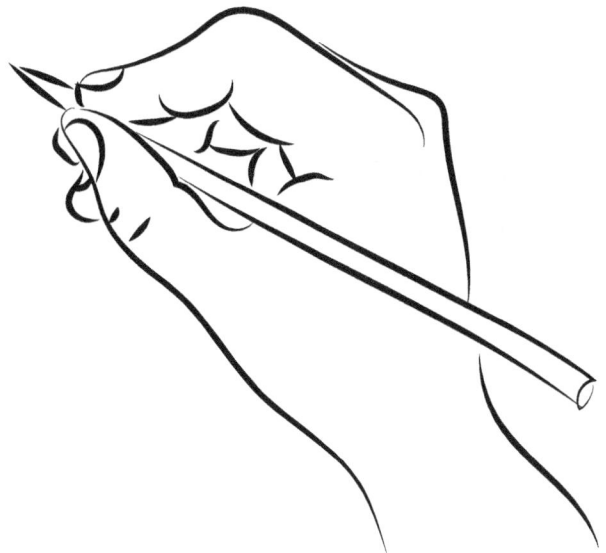

The imagery of a crown of beauty in Isaiah 62:3-5 reveals how deeply God values and esteems His daughters. Underline or highlight any words that stand out to you.

ISAIAH 62:3-5

You are a crown of beauty!

"You shall be a crown of beauty in the hand of the Lord, and a royal diadem in the hand of your God."

_____

_____

_____

_____

_____

_____

_____

_____

Reflection: Write down what it means to you to be a "crown of beauty" in God's hand.

Action Step: Create a piece of art (drawing, painting, or collage) that represents this verse.

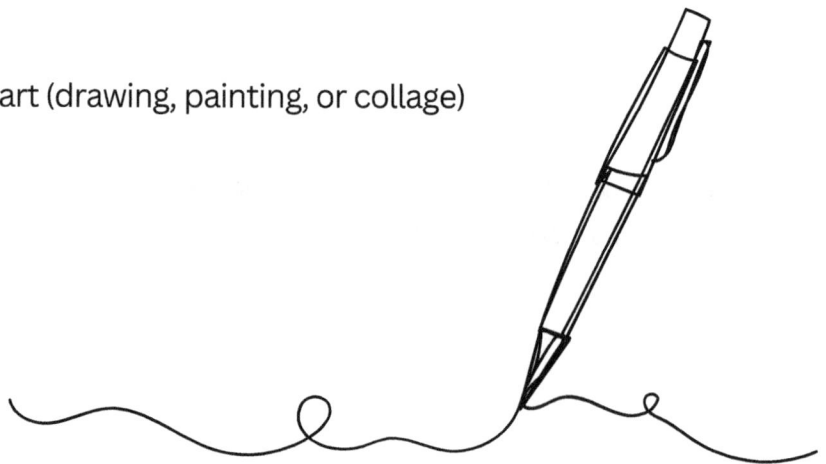

Imagine the joy and delight God experiences in you. He rejoices over you—not because of anything you've done to earn His love, but simply because you are His beloved child. Just as a loving parent delights in their child's presence, God finds joy in you, His daughter. Underline or highlight any words that stand out to you.

ZEPHANIAH 3:17

He rejoices over you with gladness

"The Lord your God is in your midst, a mighty One who will save; He will rejoice over you with gladness; He will quiet you by His love; He will exult over you with loud singing."

_____
_____
_____
_____
_____
_____
_____
_____

Reflection: Write a letter to yourself from God, expressing His joy and love for you.

Action Step: Share this verse with a friend who needs encouragement.

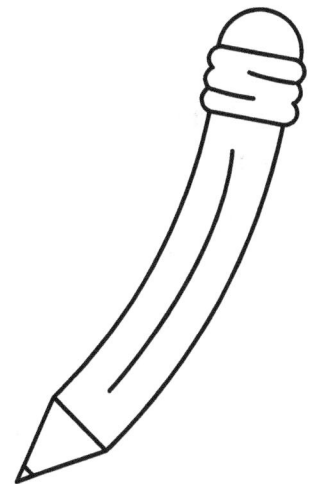

The phrase "the apple of God's eye" in Hebrew literally means "the daughter of the eye." In this context, "apple" refers to the pupil—the part of the eye where one's reflection is seen in another. This imagery emphasizes the eye's sensitivity and vulnerability, highlighting our deep need for God's protection. God watches over you with tender care and intentional love. If you could gaze into His eyes, you would see your own reflection—a beautiful daughter created in His image. Just as a mirror reflects its source, you are designed to reflect God's character, love, and glory. Underline or highlight any words that stand out to you.

LAMENTATIONS 2:18

You are the apple of God's eye!

Their heart cried unto the Lord: O wall of the daughter of Zion, let tears run down like a river day and night; Give thyself no respite; let not the apple of thine eye cease.

Reflection: Journal about a time when you felt protected by God.

Action Step: Write a prayer thanking God for His protection and care.

This verse reminds us of the depth and power of God's love for us. Nothing in all creation can separate us from the love of God that is in Christ Jesus our Lord. This profound truth offers immense comfort and unwavering assurance in our daily lives. Underline or highlight any words that stand out to you.

ROMANS 8:38-39

Nothing can separate us from God's love!

"For I am convinced that neither death nor life, neither angels nor demons, neither the present nor the future, nor any powers, neither height nor depth, nor anything else in all creation, will be able to separate us from the love of God that is in Christ Jesus our Lord."

_____

_____

_____

_____

_____

_____

_____

_____

_____

Reflection: Meditate on the fact that nothing can separate you from God's love. Write down how this assurance impacts your feelings and perspective.

Action Step: Write a letter to yourself about God's unbreakable love and read it during tough times. Share this verse with someone who needs encouragement.

Drawing close to God is an invitation to experience His presence and love more deeply. As we seek to know His character and understand His ways through prayer and His Word, we can rest in the assurance of His promises. Underline or highlight any words that stand out to you.

JAMES 4:8

Draw near to God and He will too!

"Draw near to God, and He will draw near to you."

_____
_____
_____
_____
_____
_____
_____
_____

Reflection: Write down your thoughts as you reflect on this promise and how it impacts your relationship with God.

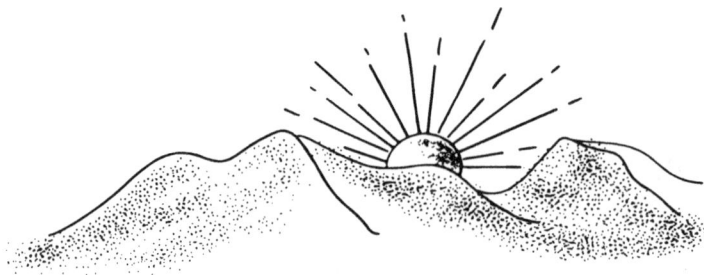

Action Step: Make a commitment to set aside specific time each day to draw near to God in prayer and reading the Bible. Observe how your connection strengthens. Share with a friend to encourage each other and be accountable.

GOD'S LOVE

As you internalize the truth of God's love, the purest expression of love imaginable, you can live confidently in the purpose for which you were created (**Ephesians 2:10**). Picture yourself embraced by Jesus, experiencing the profound security and peace of His presence (**John 14:27**). Bask in His love, demonstrated powerfully at the cross of Calvary where He made the ultimate sacrifice (**Romans 5:8**), with the assurance that nothing can snatch you from His hand (**John 10:28**). Even the Father holds you securely in His grasp. (**John 10:29**). Rest in the eternal safety of God's love, knowing nothing can separate you from it (**Romans 8:38–39**).

NOW GO AND REFLECT HIS LOVE AND GRACE TO THE WORLD AROUND YOU!

"Often, stepping into your divine assignment means *stepping out of your comfort zone.*"

Victoria Osteen

CHAPTER 10

Discovering Your Shared Purpose

TO KNOW HIM

Every woman shares one foundational purpose—to know God through Jesus Christ. This relationship is not merely for receiving blessings but for living a meaningful, fulfilled life rooted in intimacy with Him. God desires every woman to know Him deeply and personally. This intimacy reveals her identity as God's beloved child, anchoring her worth and value in Him, beyond societal standards. Knowing God is foundational to understanding a woman's purpose. It establishes her self-esteem in God's unconditional love, fostering security and confidence to live authentically. A relationship with God offers guidance and wisdom, enabling her to discern His will and make decisions aligned with His plan for her life. This connection also provides strength and encouragement during challenges. Moreover, knowing God enhances all relationships, allowing her to extend compassion and forgiveness to family, friends, and her community. She becomes an integral part of the body of Christ, conveying God's love to those around her.

Knowing God is essential for spiritual growth. Understanding His character strengthens her faith, draws others to Him, and enables her to reflect His glory. As she matures, she becomes equipped to fulfill her divine calling and impact the world.

To know God is to understand His attributes: *His love* (**1 John 4:8**), *mercy* (**Ephesians 2:4**), *justice* (**Deuteronomy 32:4**), *faithfulness* (**1 Corinthians 1:9**), *wisdom* (**Romans 11:33**), and *holiness* (**1 Peter 1:16**). These qualities reveal His worthiness and inspire her to pursue a life of purity and righteousness. His love and compassion give her a sense of belonging and value, while His mercy and forgiveness are boundless. His justice prevails, His faithfulness endures, His wisdom guides her decisions, and His holiness encourages righteous living. God is a just God, fairer than any earthly judge. His faithfulness endures through every trial, and He never abandons her. His wisdom guides her through life's difficult decisions, while His holiness inspires her to pursue purity. Knowing that God understands her imperfections and forgives her when she confesses her sins reassures her of His love and mercy. Unlike the control experienced in abuse, God respects her free will, gently guiding her into His truth and purpose with love and patience. He understands her pain and provides comfort and healing at her pace, helping her trust and follow His lead without fear or pressure.

This transformation is pivotal—not only for her life but also for those around her. As she grows in the knowledge of God, she is equipped to serve Him by serving others, sharing the love and hope she has found. God desires women to know Him deeply so they can live a life rich in purpose, reflecting His glory.

The following pages contain Bible verses that highlight God's invitation to seek and know Him, emphasizing relationship, understanding, and obedience in our faith journey.

Now this is eternal life: that they know You, the only true God, and Jesus Christ, whom You have sent.

~John 17:3

GOD AS RELATIONSHIP-SEEKER

GOD PROMISES HIS PRESENCE TO THOSE WHO DRAW NEAR

God promises a reciprocal relationship—when we move toward Him, He moves toward us with His presence. "*Come near to God and He will come near to you. Wash your hands, you sinners, and purify your hearts, you double-minded.*" **James 4:8**

GOD DESIRES INTIMATE KNOWLEDGE, NOT JUST RITUAL

God values a heartfelt relationship and true knowledge of Him over religious rituals performed without genuine love. "*For I desire mercy, not sacrifice, and acknowledgment of God rather than burnt offerings.*" **Hosea 6:6**

GOD TAKES INITIATIVE IN REVEALING HIMSELF

God takes the first step in establishing relationship, actively working to create in us the capacity to know Him. "*I will give them a heart to know me, that I am the Lord. They will be my people, and I will be their God, for they will return to me with all their heart.*" **Jeremiah 24:7**

GOD DEFINES ETERNAL LIFE AS KNOWING HIM

Eternal life and salvation are defined as an intimate, personal knowledge of God through Jesus Christ. "*Now this is eternal life: that they know you, the only true God, and Jesus Christ, whom you have sent.*" **John 17:3**

GOD REWARDS THOSE WHO DILIGENTLY SEEK HIM

God promises that those who earnestly pursue knowing Him will find Him.
"*Indeed, if you call out for insight and cry aloud for understanding, and if you look for it as for silver and search for it as for hidden treasure, then you will understand the fear of the Lord and find the knowledge of God.*" **Proverbs 2:3-5**

GOD INVITES PERSONAL REVELATION THROUGH STILLNESS

God reveals Himself most clearly when we quiet ourselves before Him, creating space to recognize His sovereignty.
"*He says, 'Be still, and know that I am God; I will be exalted among the nations, I will be exalted in the earth.'*" **Psalm 46:10**

GOD VALUES GROWTH IN RELATIONSHIP

God desires a dynamic and deepening relationship with us that continues to mature throughout our lives.
"*But grow in the grace and knowledge of our Lord and Savior Jesus Christ. To Him be glory both now and forever! Amen.*" **2 Peter 3:18**

GOD DESIRES OBEDIENCE AS EVIDENCE OF RELATIONSHIP

True knowledge of God naturally produces obedience; our actions reveal whether we genuinely know Him.
"*We know that we have come to know Him if we keep His commands. Whoever says, 'I know Him,' but does not do what He commands is a liar, and the truth is not in that person.*" **1 John 2:3-4**

GOD'S ATTRIBUTES
COMPASSIONATE

Psalm 103:13: *"As a father has compassion on his children, so the Lord has compassion on those who fear Him."*

COUNSELOR

Isaiah 9:6: *"For to us a child is born, to us a Son is given, and the government will be on His shoulders. And He will be called Wonderful Counselor, Mighty God, Everlasting Father, Prince of Peace."*

CREATOR

Genesis 1:1: *"In the beginning God created the heavens and the earth."*

ETERNAL AND EVERLASTING

Isaiah 40:28: *"Do you not know? Have you not heard? The Lord is the everlasting God, the Creator of the ends of the earth. He will not grow tired or weary, and his understanding no one can fathom."*

FAITHFUL

1 Corinthians 1:9: *"God is faithful, who has called you into fellowship with His Son, Jesus Christ our Lord."*

FORGIVING

1 John 1:9: *"If we confess our sins, He is faithful and just and will forgive us our sins and purify us from all unrighteousness."*

FORTRESS

Psalm 91:2: *"I will say of the Lord, 'He is my refuge and my fortress, my God, in whom I trust.'"*

GOOD

Psalm 34:8: *"Taste and see that the Lord is good; blessed is the one who takes refuge in Him."*

GRACIOUS

Exodus 34:6: *"And He passed in front of Moses, proclaiming, 'The Lord, the Lord, the compassionate and gracious God, slow to anger, abounding in love and faithfulness."*

HEALER

Exodus 15:26: *"He said, 'If you listen carefully to the Lord your God and do what is right in His eyes, if you pay attention to His commands and keep all His decrees, I will not bring on you any of the diseases I brought on the Egyptians, for I am the Lord, who heals you.'"*

Helper

Psalm 54:4: *"Surely God is my help; the Lord is the one who sustains me."*

Holy

1 Peter 1:16: *"For it is written: 'Be holy, because I am holy.'"*

Immutable (Unchanging)

Hebrews 13:8: *"Jesus Christ is the same yesterday and today and forever."*

Jealous

Exodus 34:14: *"Do not worship any other god, for the Lord, whose name is Jealous, is a jealous God."*

Judge

James 4:12: *"There is only one Lawgiver and Judge, the one who is able to save and destroy. But you—who are you to judge your neighbor?"*

Just

Deuteronomy 32:4: *"He is the Rock, His works are perfect, and all His ways are just. A faithful God who does no wrong, upright and just is He."*

Kind, Compassionate and Forgiving

Ephesians 4:32: *"Be kind and compassionate to one another, forgiving each other, just as in Christ God forgave you."*

Light

John 8:12: *"When Jesus spoke again to the people, He said, 'I am the light of the world. Whoever follows Me will never walk in darkness, but will have the light of life.'"*

Long-Suffering

Exodus 34:6: *"And He passed in front of Moses, proclaiming, 'The Lord, the Lord, the compassionate and gracious God, slow to anger, abounding in love and faithfulness.'"*

Love

1 John 4:8: "Anyone who does not love does not know God, because God is love."

Majestic

Psalm 8:1: "Lord, our Lord, how majestic is your name in all the earth! You have set your glory in the heavens."

Merciful

Ephesians 2:4: "But because of His great love for us, God, who is rich in mercy."

OMNIPOTENT (ALL-POWERFUL)

Jeremiah 32:17: *"Ah, Sovereign LORD, You have made the heavens and the earth by your great power and outstretched arm. Nothing is too hard for you."*

OMNIPRESENT (EVERYWHERE)

Psalm 139:7-8: *"Where can I go from your Spirit? Where can I flee from your presence? If I go up to the heavens, you are there; if I make my bed in the depths, you are there."*

OMNISCIENT (ALL-KNOWING)

Psalm 147:5: *"Great is our Lord and mighty in power; His understanding has no limit."*

PATIENT

2 Peter 3:9: *"The Lord is not slow in keeping His promise, as some understand slowness. Instead He is patient with you, not wanting anyone to perish, but everyone to come to repentance."*

PEACE

Philippians 4:7: *"And the peace of God, which transcends all understanding, will guard your hearts and your minds in Christ Jesus."*

PROTECTOR

Psalm 91:1-2: *"Whoever dwells in the shelter of the Most High will rest in the shadow of the Almighty. I will say of the LORD, 'He is my refuge and my fortress, my God, in whom I trust.'"*

PROVIDER

Philippians 4:19: *"And my God will meet all your needs according to the riches of His glory in Christ Jesus."*

REDEEMER

Isaiah 44:22: "I have swept away your offenses like a cloud, your sins like the morning mist. Return to me, for I have redeemed you."

REFUGE

Psalm 46:1: "God is our refuge and strength, an ever-present help in trouble."

RIGHTEOUS

Psalm 145:17: "The Lord is righteous in all His ways and faithful in all He does."

ROCK

Deuteronomy 32:4: "He is the Rock, His works are perfect, and all His ways are just. A faithful God who does no wrong, upright and just is He."

SANCTIFIER

Hebrews 10:14: *"For by one sacrifice He has made perfect forever those who are being made holy."*

SHEPHERD

Psalm 23:1: *"The Lord is my shepherd, I lack nothing."*

SOVEREIGN

1 Chronicles 29:11: *"Yours, Lord, is the greatness and the power and the glory and the majesty and the splendor, for everything in heaven and earth is yours. Yours, Lord, is the kingdom; you are exalted as head over all."*

SUSTAINER

Colossians 1:17: *"He is before all things, and in him all things hold together."*

TRUTH

John 14:6: *"Jesus answered, 'I am the way and the truth and the life. No one comes to the Father except through me.'"*

WISE

Romans 11:33: *"Oh, the depth of the riches of the wisdom and knowledge of God! How unsearchable His judgments, and His paths beyond tracing out!"*

God is with me always

WHO IS GOD

God reveals His true nature through His various names. Studying these names provides valuable insight into His character, much like understanding our identity in Christ reveals the truth about who we are. The more we learn about God through His names and His Word, the deeper our intimacy with Him becomes. Just as conversing with God strengthens our personal relationship with Him, understanding His character through His names draws us closer to His heart.

It's not just about acquiring knowledge of God; it's about responding to Him with reverence and awe for His authentic self. When we recognize God as He declares Himself to be, we can also trust that we are who He says we are. This understanding is foundational to discovering our purpose in His Kingdom.

The more we come to know God through His names, the deeper our understanding of His nature becomes. This, in turn, fosters a greater reverence and relationship with Him.

Below are some names of God that hold particular significance for us as women:

El-Shaddai: Meaning "God Almighty" or "God of the Mountains," El-Shaddai emphasizes God's power, sufficiency, and provision. As women, we can find strength and comfort in knowing that God is our source of strength and sustenance.

Jehovah-Rapha: This name means "The Lord Who Heals" and speaks to God's ability to bring healing and restoration. It assures women that God cares for their physical, emotional, and spiritual well-being, offering healing to every aspect of their lives.

Jehovah-Jireh: Translated as "The Lord Will Provide," this name reminds us that God is our provider. It builds trust in His faithfulness to meet our needs, both material and spiritual, and encourages us to rely on Him for provision in every area of life.

Jehovah-Shalom: Meaning "The Lord Is Peace," Jehovah-Shalom reassures us that God can bring peace in the midst of life's storms. It offers comfort to women, reminding them that true peace and rest are found in God's presence, no matter the circumstances.

Jehovah-Nissi: "The Lord Is My Banner" or "The Lord Is My Victory" signifies God's role as our protector and guide. He leads us to victory over life's challenges and enemies, empowering us to trust in His strength and guidance through every battle.

El-Roi: Translated as "The God Who Sees Me," this name brings women assurance that God intimately sees them and knows them personally. It is a reminder that we are never alone, and our struggles and pain are never hidden from God's sight.

Abba: Though not a traditional Hebrew name, "Abba" is a term of endearment used by Jesus, meaning "Father" or "Daddy." This name reflects God's loving and nurturing nature, inviting women to approach Him with childlike trust, intimacy, and confidence.

Names of God

ABBA FATHER   ADONAI THE LORD   ADVOCATE   ALMIGHTY   ALL IN ALL ALPHA   AMEN ANCIENT OF DAYS   ANOINTED ONE   APOSTLE   ARM OF THE LORD   AUTHOR OF ETERNAL SALVATION AUTHOR OF OUR FAITH   AUTHOR OF PEACE   AVENGER   BEGINNING   BISHOP OF SOULS   BLESSED   BRANCH BREAD OF LIFE   BREATH OF LIFE   BRIDEGROOM   BRIGHT MORNING STAR BUCKLER   CAPTAIN OF SALVATION   CARPENTER   CHIEF SHEPHERD CHOSEN ONE   CHRIST   COMFORTER   COMMANDER   CONSOLATION OF ISRAEL CONSUMING FIRE   CORNERSTONE   COUNSELOR   CREATOR   CROWN OF BEAUTY   DAYSPRING   DELIVERER   DIADEM OF BEAUTY   DOOR   DWELLING PLACE   ELECT ONE   EL-CHUWL   EL-DEAH   EL ELYON   EL-GIBHOR   ELOHIM EL-OLAM   EL ROI   EL-SHADDA   EMMANUEL   END   ETERNAL GOD ETERNAL LIFE   ETERNAL SPIRIT   EVERLASTING FATHER   EVERLASTING GOD EXCELLENT   FAITHFUL & TRUE   FAITHFUL WITNESS   FIRST AND THE LAST FIRSTBORN   FIRSTFRUITS   FORTRESS   FOUNDATION   FOUNTAIN OF LIVING WATERS   FRIEND OF SINNERS   FULLERS' SOAP   GENTLE WHISPER   GLORY OF THE LORD   GOOD SHEPHERD   GOVERNOR   GREAT HIGH PRIEST   GREAT SHEPHERD   GUIDE   HIDING PLACE   HIGH PRIEST   HOLY ONE OF ISRAEL HOLY SPIRIT   HOPE   HORN OF SALVATION   HUSBAND   I AM WHO I AM IMMANUEL   INTERCESSOR   JAH   JEALOUS   JEHOVAH   JEHOVAH JIREH JEHOVAH NISSI   JEHOVAH RAPHA   JEHOVAH ROHI   JEHOVAH SHALOM JEHOVAH SHAMMAH   JEHOVAH TSIDKENU   JESUS CHRIST   JUDGE JUST ONE   KEEPER   KING OF KINGS   LAMB OF GOD   LAST ADAM   LAWGIVER LEADER   LIFE   LIGHT OF THE WORLD   LILY OF THE VALLEY   LION OF THE TRIBE OF JUDAH   LORD OF LORDS   MAN OF SORROWS   MASTER MEDIATOR   MESSIAH   MIGHTY   NAZARENE   OFFSPRING OF DAVID OMEGA   ONLY BEGOTTEN SON PHYSICIAN   PORTION   POTTER   PRINCE OF PEACE   PROPHET   PROPITIATION   PURIFIER   REDEEMER   REFINER'S FIRE REFUGE   RESURRECTION   REWARDER   RIGHTEOUS ONE   ROCK   ROOT OF DAVID   ROSE OF SHARON   RULER   SAVIOR   SCEPTRE   SEED   SERVANT SHADE   SHEPHERD   SHIELD   STRENGTH   STONE   STRONGHOLD   STRONG TOWER   TEACHER   TEMPLE   TRUTH   VINE   WALL OF FIRE   WAY   WISDOM OF GOD   WITNESS   WONDERFUL   WORD   YAH   YAHWEH   YAHWEH-GHMOLAH   YAHWEH-MACCADDESHEM   YAHWEH-ROHI

MAKE HIM KNOWN

Every woman shares a foundational purpose—to make Jesus known through discipleship. As **Acts 1:8** declares: "*But you will receive power when the Holy Spirit has come upon you, and you will be my witnesses in Jerusalem and in all Judea and Samaria, and to the end of the earth.*"

Sharing Jesus with others is a mandate given to all believers and brings glory to God. When we testify to His goodness and share the gospel, we extend His love and truth. Evangelism is not just a duty; it's a heartfelt response to God's grace, reflecting our desire to see others come to know Him. As women of purpose, we are called to be a light in the darkness, to bring hope to the hopeless, and to lead others to the saving knowledge of Jesus Christ. By doing so, we fulfill the Great Commission and honor God with our lives.

As believers empowered by the Holy Spirit, our mandate to share the gospel stems from **Acts 1:8**, where Jesus promises His followers will receive power to be His witnesses throughout the world. This commission is not just a task; it's a privilege and calling—an opportunity to magnify God's glory by proclaiming His love and salvation. When we boldly testify to His goodness and grace, we participate in the divine work of bringing others into a life-changing relationship with Him.

How do we do that? The easiest way is not through a formula or method but by sharing what Jesus has done in our lives. What has He changed for you? Have you experienced less anxiety, more peace, or freedom from addiction? Sharing your testimony, especially with those who knew you before your salvation, is a powerful proof of Christ's transformative power. Every person we reach becomes a living testimony to God's ability to change lives and His desire for all to experience His love.

Evangelism is both a responsibility and a joyous response to the immense love God has lavished upon us. It's an act of compassion for those who are lost and a demonstration of our obedience to Christ's commandments. As women of purpose, we embody God's heart for the world, shining His light in dark places, offering hope where there is despair, and guiding others into the liberating truth of the gospel. Through our words and actions, we reflect the love and compassion of Jesus Christ, inviting others to encounter His grace and mercy.

By fulfilling the Great Commission, we honor God with our lives and contribute to His kingdom-building work. Each soul we lead to Christ is a precious addition to God's family, a testimony to His faithfulness and redemptive power. Our commitment to evangelism is rooted in gratitude for God's salvation and a deep desire to see His kingdom expand. When we share Jesus with others, we join in the ongoing story of God's love for humanity, inviting people from all nations and backgrounds to receive the gift of eternal life through faith in Christ.

THE GREAT COMMISSION: OUR CORE MANDATE

"*Jesus came and said to them, 'All authority in heaven and on earth has been given to me. Go therefore and make disciples of all nations, baptizing them in the name of the Father and Son and of the Holy Spirit, teaching them to observe all that I have commanded you. And behold, I am with you always, to the end of the age.'*" **Matthew 28:18-20**

GLOBAL GOSPEL PROCLAMATION

"*And He said to them, 'Go into all the world and proclaim the gospel to the whole creation.*" **Mark 16:15**

MESSAGE OF REPENTANCE AND FORGIVENESS

"*...thus it is written, that the Christ should suffer and on the third day rise from the dead, and that repentance for the forgiveness of sins should be proclaimed in His name to all nations, beginning from Jerusalem.'* **Luke 24:46-47**

THE NECESSITY OF EVANGELISM

"*How then will they call on Him in whom they have not believed? And how are they to believe in Him of whom they have never heard? And how are they to hear without someone preaching? And how are they to preach unless they are sent? As it is written, 'How beautiful are the feet of those who preach the good news!'*" **Romans 10:14-15**

MINISTRY OF RECONCILIATION

"*All this is from God, who through Christ reconciled us to Himself and gave us the ministry of reconciliation; that is, in Christ God was reconciling the world to Himself, not counting their trespasses against them, and entrusting to us the message of reconciliation. Therefore, we are ambassadors for Christ, God making His appeal through us. We implore you on behalf of Christ, be reconciled to God.*" **2 Corinthians 5:18-20**

PERSONAL TESTIMONY WITH GRACE

"*But in your hearts honor Christ the Lord as holy, always being prepared to make a defense to anyone who asks you for a reason for the hope that is in you; yet do it with gentleness and respect.*" **1 Peter 3:15**

CONTINUING CHRIST'S MISSION

"*Jesus said to them again, 'Peace be with you. As the Father has sent me, even so I am sending you.'*" **John 20:21**

WITNESS THROUGH GODLY LIVING

"*You are the light of the world. A city set on a hill cannot be hidden. Nor do people light a lamp and put it under a basket, but on a stand, and it gives light to all in the house. In the same way, let your light shine before others, so that they may see your good works and give glory to your Father who is in heaven.*" **Matthew 5:14-16**

FAITHFUL TEACHING AND EXHORTATION

"*Preach the word; be ready in season and out of season; reprove, rebuke, and exhort, with complete patience and teaching.*" **2 Timothy 4:2**

PRAYER FOR BOLDNESS IN SHARING THE GOSPEL

Lord Jesus, I pray that You would give me the words to speak when I open my mouth, boldly proclaiming the mystery of the Gospel, for which I am an ambassador. Grant me the courage and boldness to speak Your truth without fear or hesitation. Help me to speak the truth in love, to be salt that doesn't lose its flavor, and to shine as a light in the darkness for those who do not yet know You.

Give me wisdom and discernment as I share the Gospel, that I may effectively reach those who are lost. As I live my life for You, Jesus, help me to reach out with hands, heart, and life to those who need comfort—whether the poor in spirit or the poor in material need.

Help me to fearlessly proclaim Your Word, and give me the grace to be a living example of Your love and grace. I trust that the power of Your Word changes lives, and that Your Holy Spirit draws people to You. When Your message is not received, give me the strength to shake the dust off my feet and move on, always trusting in Your plan.

Forgive me when I am too timid, and when I make excuses out of fear or hesitancy. Empower me to speak boldly in the power of Your Holy Spirit, for the glory of Your name, and out of love for my Lord and Savior, Jesus Christ. I pray that many will come to know You through my efforts, and that Your Kingdom will be expanded as a result.

Use me, Lord, however You choose, to further Your Kingdom, for Your Kingdom is not of this world. Help me to be set apart, anointed, and willing to be a vessel for Your use. Let Your love overflow from me, as I drink from Your eternal well, and may rivers of life flow through me to those around me.

Use the trauma and wounds You've allowed in my life to give me a heart for the lost, and to show Your compassion and mercy. You have said that You want none to perish, but for all to come to salvation. I lift up lost souls everywhere, and pray for Your Kingdom to come and for Your will to be done on earth as it is in heaven.

In the mighty name of Jesus, I pray. Amen.

OUR PERSONAL TESTIMONY

Our personal testimony—the story of God's work in our lives—serves as one of the most powerful ways we fulfill our purpose of glorifying God and making Him known. Unlike general evangelism, our testimony offers a deeply personal witness to God's transformative power. Scripture repeatedly highlights the importance and strength of sharing what God has done in our lives.

THE UNIQUE POWER OF A WOMAN'S TESTIMONY

"Many of the Samaritans from that town believed in him because of the woman's testimony..." **John 4:39** The Samaritan woman, with a complicated past and marginalized status, led an entire community to Jesus through her simple, honest testimony. This shows how God can use any woman's story—regardless of her background or limitations—to draw others to Christ. Throughout history, women's testimonies have opened doors where formal preaching could not. In many cultures, a woman sharing her personal experience creates a unique bridge for the gospel.

"And they overcame him by the blood of the Lamb and by the word of their testimony, and they did not love their lives to the death." **Revelation 12:11** This verse reveals that our testimony holds spiritual authority. When combined with the blood of Jesus, our personal witness becomes a weapon that defeats the enemy. Our stories are not just inspiring—they carry divine power.

"Let the redeemed of the Lord tell their story—those he redeemed from the hand of the foe." **Psalm 107:2**

God specifically calls those He has redeemed to declare His work. Our testimony is not optional—it's a divine invitation to participate in God's ongoing story of redemption.

"Go home to your own people and tell them how much the Lord has done for you, and how he has had mercy on you." **Mark 5:19**

After delivering a man from severe demonic oppression, Jesus didn't invite him to join the disciples. Instead, He commissioned him to go home and testify. This shows that sharing our story in our existing relationships and communities is a high calling.

BEYOND FORMULAS: THE POWER OF PERSONAL EXPERIENCE

While evangelism methods like the Romans Road, the Four Spiritual Laws, or the Bridge Illustration can be helpful tools, Scripture emphasizes that our personal testimony carries unique spiritual power that formulas alone cannot replicate. Jesus didn't instruct the healed demoniac to memorize a gospel presentation—He told him to share what God had done for him. Similarly, the Samaritan woman didn't present a theological outline—she simply said, *"Come see a man who told me everything I ever did."*

THE SPIRITUAL POWER OF YOUR TESTIMONY

What makes your testimony so powerful? It's the objective truth of the gospel combined with the subjective reality of a changed life. It's the authentic voice of someone the hearer often already knows and trusts. While evangelism methods may change with time and culture, the power of personal testimony transcends these boundaries. When we share our story, we're not just presenting information—we're inviting others to experience the living reality of Christ's work. Scripture emphasizes testimony as a primary means of spreading the gospel, and the Holy Spirit works through our honest, heartfelt accounts in ways that even the most carefully crafted presentations cannot match. Your story becomes living evidence of God's ongoing work in the world today. Your story is the redemptive work of Jesus on the cross, carried with you and within you.

THE POWER IN YOUR STORY

Revelation 12:11 speaks of overcoming by "*the blood of the Lamb and the word of their testimony,*" revealing the unique spiritual power your story carries in these ways:

Spiritual Authority: When we share what God has done in our lives, we're not just telling a story—we're making a declaration backed by the finished work of Christ. Our testimony carries spiritual weight because it's anchored in Christ's victory, not just our experience.

Breaking Strongholds: When someone hears how God delivered you from addiction, healed your marriage, or transformed your thinking, it directly challenges the enemy's lies that such freedom is impossible. Your real-life story shows that Satan's power has limitations.

Living Proof: The enemy wants people to believe that following Christ doesn't make a difference. Your testimony provides tangible evidence that contradicts this lie. It demonstrates the reality of God's transforming power in everyday life.

Faith-Building Power: Testimonies build faith in others by showing God's faithfulness in specific situations. When someone struggling with similar issues hears how God worked in your life, it creates hope and expectation that God can do the same for them.

Overcoming Shame: Many people remain in bondage because shame keeps them silent. When we openly share our stories—especially our struggles—we demonstrate that God's redemption is greater than our shame, opposing the enemy's strategy of isolation.

Declaring Truth: Testimony is a form of truth-telling that directly counters Satan, who is described as "*the father of lies*" **John 8.:44**. Speaking truth about God's work in our lives dispels darkness and deception.

Your testimony isn't just an inspirational anecdote—it's a spiritual declaration. When rooted in Christ's sacrifice, it actively participates in God's ongoing victory over evil. Your story becomes part of God's redemptive narrative, continually defeating the enemy's purposes.

ELEMENTS OF A POWERFUL TESTIMONY

Testimonies come in many forms. If you came to Christ as a child, focus on significant moments of growth and God's faithfulness through different life seasons. Whether your story is dramatic or quiet, sudden or gradual, it matters. God uses all kinds of stories to draw people to Himself.

Your Life Before Christ: Share your life before Jesus, but avoid glamorizing sin. Instead, focus on the struggles or emptiness you experienced without Him.

How You Encountered Jesus: Highlight the circumstances and the turning point when you encountered Christ. What led you to Him?

The Transformation He's Brought: Explain how your life has changed—your thoughts, behaviors, and relationships. What areas of your life have been transformed by God's power?

Your Ongoing Journey: Be honest about your continued growth. Share victories and the areas where God is still working in your life.

PRACTICAL WAYS TO SHARE YOUR TESTIMONY

Be prepared to share your story at any moment. 1 Peter 3:15 "*Always be prepared to give an answer to everyone who asks you to give the reason for the hope that you have.*"

Keep it concise. Practice sharing your story in 3-5 minutes for everyday opportunities

Speak their language: Adapt your vocabulary for your audience; especially for those unfamiliar with church terminology

Make it about Jesus. While it's your story, make sure Christ remains the hero. Share with gentleness as your testimony is an invitation, not an argument.

WHEN TO SHARE YOUR TESTIMONY

When someone asks about a change they've noticed in your life

When someone shares a struggle similar to one God has helped you overcome

During times of crisis when others need hope

In small group settings, where vulnerability creates connection

When mentoring or discipling others

In formal ministry settings when appropriate

Through writing—journals, blogs, newsletters, music, art, poetry, etc.

OVERCOMING BARRIERS TO SHARING YOUR STORY

Many believers hesitate to share their testimony because of the following barriers:

Fear of rejection or judgment

Concern about not being "eloquent enough"

Feeling their story isn't dramatic or significant

Shame about past sins or ongoing struggles

Uncertainty about what details to include

The power of your testimony doesn't depend on your eloquence or the dramatic nature of your story—it depends on God's Holy Spirit, His faiithfulness and what Jesus has done.

REFLECTION QUESTIONS TO WRITE YOUR TESTIMONY ON THE NEXT PAGE

Use the space on the next page to write a brief (3-5 minute) version of your testimony, incorporating your responses to the following questions

1. What was the specific moment or season when you first recognized your need for Jesus?
2. What were the circumstances surrounding this time?
3. When did you give your life to Jesus Christ?
4. Describe the moment or decision.
5. What emotions or thoughts followed your commitment to Christ?
6. What specific ways has God transformed your life that would resonate with others?
7. Consider areas such as your mindset, actions, or relationships.
8. Which parts of your testimony most clearly display God's character and power?
9. Focus on the aspects that show His faithfulness, love, and strength.
10. Name 3-5 specific ways your life has changed since following Christ.
11. Think about changes in relationships, thought patterns, habits, or priorities.
12. What is one struggle that God has helped you overcome or is helping you navigate?
13. How specifically did or does His presence make a difference?
14. What scripture verse became especially meaningful during your journey with Christ?
15. Why did it impact you, and how has it shaped your faith?
16. If you could share just one thing about what Jesus has done in your life with someone who doesn't know Him, what would it be?
17. What misconceptions did you have about God before you truly encountered Him?
18. How has your understanding changed?
19. How has God's faithfulness been evident during your most challenging seasons?
20. What would your life look like today if you hadn't encountered Christ?
21. When have you experienced God's presence most powerfully?
22. What happened, and how did it affect you?
23. What parts of your testimony might especially resonate with someone who is struggling or searching right now?
24. Who in your circle of influence might especially benefit from hearing your story?
25. What holds you back from sharing your testimony more freely?
26. Identify any fears or barriers.
27. How could you incorporate your testimony naturally into your everyday conversations?
28. Think of practical ways to share it with others.

LOVING GOD

Mark 12:30 "*And you shall love the Lord your God with all your heart, with all your soul, with all your mind, and with all your strength. This is the first commandment.* "

When Jesus was asked about the greatest commandment, He quoted directly from the Shema, the central prayer in Jewish tradition found in **Deuteronomy 6:4-5**. The Shema begins with "*Hear, O Israel: The LORD our God, the LORD is one!*" and continues with the command to love God with our entire being which is a command that reveals a foundational shared purpose as believers: to love God completely with every aspect of our being. Let's explore the rich meaning behind these Hebrew words:

Ahavah (אֲהַב) - **Love** In Hebrew isn't merely emotional but encompasses devotion, loyalty, and commitment. It's an action that manifests in obedience and service. This love isn't optional—it's commanded—showing love can be both a feeling and a choice we make.

Lebab (לֵבָב) - **Heart** In Hebrew represents more than emotions; it's the center of thinking, decision-making, and will. To love God with all your heart means He becomes the focus of your decisions, desires, and intentions—the central priority of your entire inner life.

Nephesh (נֶפֶשׁ) - **Soul/Life** in Hebrew refers to your entire being, your very life essence. It encompasses your identity, personality, and the core of who you are. Loving God with all your soul means dedicating your entire identity and existence to Him.

Meod (מְאֹד) - **Very Much/Strength** translated as "strength," meod literally means "very much" or "exceedingly." It refers to loving God with all your resources, energy, and abilities —holding nothing back in your devotion to Him.

Practical Application: Loving God completely means:

Prioritizing relationship with Him above all else

Studying His Word to know Him more deeply

Obeying His commands out of love, not obligation

Worshiping Him with sincere praise

Surrendering your resources, time, and talents to His purposes

Reflection Questions:

Which aspect of loving God (heart, soul, mind, strength) comes most naturally to you?

Which aspect presents the greatest challenge?

What practical step can you take today to grow in your love for God?

Prayer: Father, deepen my love for You. May I love You with my whole being—heart, soul, mind, and strength—not just through words but through a life of devotion. In Jesus' name, Amen.

TO LOVE OUR NEIGHBOR

Mark 12:31 *"And the second, like it, is this: You shall love your neighbor as yourself. There is no other commandment greater than these."* The second part of this command is to love our neighbors; another shared purpose as believers. When Jesus taught about loving our neighbors, He included a profound truth many believers overlook—we must also add "as yourself". This is not about selfish pride, but a sacred recognition that we too are beloved children of God. I used to walk through life with deep self-hatred, pouring out what I thought was love to others while remaining empty and void of a self inside. Through dissociation from trauma, I had a fractured sense of self and a distorted understanding of love. I misunderstood the biblical call to selflessness. God never intended for anyone to be an empty temple or hollow vessel. Through much healing, prayer and God's Word, I began to understand how much God truly loved me. As His truths penetrated the broken places in my heart, my fractured self began to heal. **Ephesians 3:17-19** became my prayer: *"That Christ may dwell in your hearts through faith; that you, being rooted and grounded in love, may be able to comprehend with all the saints what is the width and length and depth and height—to know the love of Christ which passes knowledge; that you may be filled with all the fullness of God."* Only then could I love with Christ's genuine love rather than from people-pleasing or performance. Jesus helped me reclaim my mind, emotions, body, and soul and become more whole. Then I had a sense of self to receive God's love and to love others as myself. Jesus said we should *"love your neighbor as yourself"*—not instead of yourself. This assumes a healthy love of self based on understanding our value in God's eyes and His love for us as His creation. Christ's command to *"love your neighbor as yourself"* transforms from duty to delight as we become conduits of His endless grace, loving others authentically without losing ourselves because our source is infinite. In this we find fulfillment and divine purpose in an outpouring that never depletes us.

Scripture reveals a divine pattern for love:

1. God loves us first **1 John 4:19**
2. We receive and accept His love
3. We learn to see ourselves through His eyes
4. From this fullness, we love others from the overflow

Reflection Questions:

- In what ways do you struggle to accept God's love for yourself?
- How might your ability to love others change if you first received God's love fully?
- Who is the "neighbor" God is calling you to love from this place of fullness?

Prayer: *Lord, heal the broken places in me that prevent me from receiving Your love. Help me to love myself from a grateful humble acceptance as Your creation and be able to love my neighbors from the fullness of the love You have for me. In Jesus' name, Amen.*

"A woman's purpose isn't found in perfection, performance, or pleasing others—*it's found in knowing she is loved by God and living from that love to help others heal.*"
Sharri Burggraaf

FURTHER PURPOSES WITHIN SCRIPTURE

The Bible tells us that knowing God through Jesus and making disciples is our ultimate purpose. The Scriptures also clearly outline key purposes that apply to all believers.

SINGLENESS

Scripture honors singleness as a gift that allows undivided devotion to the Lord. "*I wish that all of you were as I am. But each of you has your own gift from God; one has this gift, another has that. Now to the unmarried and the widows I say: It is good for them to stay unmarried, as I do*" **1 Corinthians 7:7-8**.

MARRIAGE

God instituted marriage between one man and one woman as a sacred covenant. "*That is why a man leaves his father and mother and is united to his wife, and they become one flesh*" **Genesis 2:24**, commanding them to "*be fruitful and multiply*" **Genesis 1:28**. For many, especially women, marriage and motherhood can be central to God's purposes.

TRAINING CHILDREN UP IN THE LORD

Parents are entrusted with the sacred responsibility of spiritual formation. "*Start children off on the way they should go, and even when they are old they will not turn from it*" **Proverbs 22:6**.

WORK DILIGENTLY

Our work is to be done with excellence as service to the Lord, not to please people. "*Whatever you do, work at it with all your heart, as working for the Lord, not for human masters*" **Colossians 3:23**. The bible shows women serving God in diverse capacities, like Deborah as a judge or Lydia as a businesswoman.

WORSHIP GOD

We are created to worship God in spirit and truth as a lifestyle. "*Yet a time is coming and has now come when the true worshipers will worship the Father in the Spirit and in truth, for they are the kind of worshipers the Father seeks*" **John 4:23-24** and "*offer our bodies as living sacrifices in spiritual worship*" **Romans 12:1**. This worship extends beyond formal religious settings into a lifestyle that honors God in every aspect.

PURSUE JUSTICE AND MERCY

The Bible calls us to "*pursue justice and show mercy*" **Micah 6:8**, standing up for the vulnerable and marginalized in our society. Throughout Scripture, God's heart for the orphan, widow, poor, and foreigner is evident, and He invites us to share in His compassionate concern.

GLORIFY GOD IN EVERYTHING

Ultimately, whether through family life, career, ministry, all believers have a purpose to "*glorify God in everything*". "*So whether you eat or drink or whatever you do, do it all for the glory of God*" **1 Corinthians 10:31**.

108

Let's Learn From Him

This book is an invitation to learn from Jesus Christ Himself. Consider the profound story of Martha and Mary (Luke 10:38–42). While Martha was busy attending to tasks, Jesus gently reminded her that Mary had chosen the better part by sitting at His feet and soaking in His life-giving words. He commended her for learning from Him. This beautifully illustrates what our Creator desires most—our presence with Him and our devotion. Your journey of discovery begins at His feet, in His presence, during moments of worship and quiet listening. As you soak in His life-giving words, He reveals more of Himself and who He created you to be.

In His presence, every woman finds her true purpose and identity

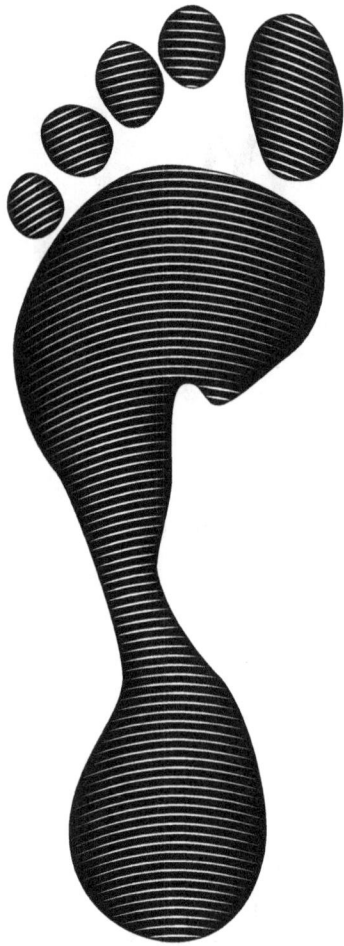

Step out of your comfort ZONE.

If I could serve God anywhere, doing anything, I would...

_____

_____

_____

_____

_____

_____

_____

CHAPTER 11

Kingdom Principles

KINGDOM PRINCIPLES

Journey through 11 Kingdom principles by focusing on truths found in Scripture. Illuminate the path to walking closer with the Lord Jesus Christ, our eternal Shepherd and lover of our souls, and knowing our God-given purpose. We find transformation and guidance by delving deeper into the truths of the Bible. These principles serve as profound beacons to guide us to align our values and beliefs with God's divine plan.

SUBMISSION

James 4:7 - *"Submit yourselves, then, to God."* Submission in God's Kingdom means willingly and voluntarily surrendering our will to God's authority. Rather than viewing it as weakness, true submission is a position of strength—recognizing God's sovereignty and aligning our desires with His. It involves letting go of self-reliance and acknowledging that His ways are higher than ours. Through submission, we find true freedom and purpose.

LOVE

1 Corinthians 13:13 - *"And now these three remain: faith, hope and love. But the greatest of these is love."* The central principle of the Kingdom of God is love, defining God's character, reflecting His heart, and ultimately His followers. Divine love (agape) goes beyond emotion to sacrificial action and unconditional acceptance. It's patient, kind, and endures all things. Love seeks the highest good of others regardless of what we receive.

JUSTICE

Isaiah 1:17 - *"Learn to do right; seek justice. Defend the oppressed."* God's Kingdom upholds justice and His perfect righteousness and reflects His concern for the vulnerable. It calls believers to stand against oppression, champion the cause of the marginalized, and work toward restoring right relationships, balancing mercy with accountability, recognizing that true healing comes when wrongs are addressed and relationships are restored.

HUMILITY

James 4:10 - *"Humble yourselves before the Lord, and he will lift you up."* Humility is an accurate self-assessment before God—recognizing both our limitations and our value as His creation. It is a key principle in God's Kingdom and means setting aside pride, embracing teachability, and acknowledging our need for God and others. Humble believers recognize their gifts, using them to serve, not elevate, themselves.

FORGIVENESS

Matthew 6:14-15 - *"For if you forgive other people...your heavenly Father will also forgive you"* Forgiveness is central to God's Kingdom. It releases others from the debt of wrongs committed against us, reflecting God's grace we've received. It doesn't minimize injustice but refuses to be defined by it. Forgiveness frees both the forgiver and the forgiven, breaking cycles of bitterness. It's a healing journey rather than a one-time event.

SERVANTHOOD

Mark 10:45 - *"For even the Son of Man did not come to be served, but to serve..."* In the Kingdom of God, greatness is found in meeting others' needs with joy and dignity. This inverts worldly power structures, defining greatness by how much we give rather than what we gain. Following Christ's example, we can serve using our strength, resources, and position to uplift others—not diminishing ourselves, but discovering His true greatness.

FAITH

Romans 1:17 - *"The righteous will live by faith."* Believers are called to a life of faith. Faith is trust in action—living according to what we believe about God's character and promises. It goes beyond intellectual assent to shape our decisions, priorities, and responses to life's challenges. Kingdom faith perseveres through uncertainty, grows through testing, and ultimately transforms how we see God, our circumstances, others, and ourselves.

HOLINESS

A hallmark of the Kingdom of God, holiness is being set apart for God's purposes, reflecting His character in every aspect of life. It involves separation from sin and dedication to righteousness. **1 Peter 1:15–16** says, *"But just as He who called you is holy, so be holy in all you do; for it is written: 'Be holy, because I am holy.'"* Holiness isn't merely rule-following but heart transformation that leads to integrity, purity of intention, and spiritual maturity—becoming who we were created to be.

GENEROSITY

2 Corinthians 9:7 - *"Each of you should give what you have decided in your heart to give..."* Generosity, a characteristic of God's Kingdom, is recognizing that everything we have comes from God's abundance. It extends beyond financial giving to sharing our time, talents, influence, and compassion. Cheerful rather than obligatory, sacrificial rather than convenient, and motivated by love rather than recognition.

UNITY

John 17:21" *...that all of them may be one, Father, just as You are in Me and I am in You"* Unity is vital in the Kingdom of God. Jesus prayed for unity among His followers so that the world may believe. Believers are called to pursue unity in the body of Christ, valuing diversity while maintaining unity in faith and purpose.

ETERNAL PERSPECTIVE

Colossians 3:2 - *"Set your minds on things above, not on earthly things."* Eternal perspective means viewing present circumstances through the lens of God's eternal, timeless Kingdom. It shifts our focus from temporary pleasures and problems to lasting spiritual realities, making decisions based on forever value.

SUBMISSION

Before exploring the 11 Kingdom principles found in the Bible, there must be a chapter dedicated solely to the topic of submission. Without an accurate biblical understanding of submitting to God, it can profoundly affect how a woman responds to Him and to all other Kingdom principles. For many women, the very mention of the word submission can evoke painful connotations—especially for those who have experienced physical, sexual, or spiritual abuse. Some religious teachings have perpetuated harmful dynamics regarding submission, both in relationship with God and within marriage. The expectation for women to be submissive and silent can deeply impact their relationship with God and influence marital dynamics, often fostering toxic environments. Misapplications of this concept have led to significant harm. Rather than being a haven, some churches have advised women to submit to their husbands regardless of the harm endured behind closed doors. In abusive situations, support for women and children within the church—as well as from law enforcement and other helping institutions—is often lacking, compounding the harm inflicted.

Misinterpretations of submission have also limited women's participation in leadership, ministry, and decision-making roles within religious settings. Many women have felt marginalized or undervalued in their faith communities, which hinders their ability to fully express their spiritual gifts and callings. These issues must be addressed before a woman can fully embrace her God-given purpose and find her rightful place in the Kingdom of God. A woman's understanding of submission plays a significant role in her ability to honor God and follow His will for her life. Some men have taken Bible verses out of context to assert authority over their wives, justify abusive behavior, and pressure women into unwanted sexual activity—even to the point of marital rape. One such passage is 1 Corinthians 7:3–5 (KJV): *"Let the husband render unto the wife due benevolence: and likewise also the wife unto the husband. The wife hath not power of her own body, but the husband: and likewise also the husband hath not power of his own body, but the wife. Defraud ye not one the other, except it be with consent for a time, that ye may give yourselves to fasting and prayer; and come together again, that Satan tempt you not for your incontinency."* The original Greek word translated as benevolence in this passage is εὔνοια (eunoia), meaning goodwill, kindness, and generosity. In Hebrew, the related concept is chesed (חֶסֶד), or lovingkindness. This reveals that Paul's instruction concerns mutual care and affection, not entitlement to physical relations. While Paul does caution against extended abstention—*"lest Satan tempt you"* (**1 Corinthians 7:5**)—this must be understood in the context of mutual agreement and consideration, never as justification for demands or coercion.

Prior to verse 3, Paul discusses how he chose to remain single so that he could give his undivided devotion to God and serve without distraction. He also recognized that not everyone has the gift of celibacy and advised those who struggled with self-control—especially amid the rampant sexual immorality in Corinth—to marry, which was God's design, rather than fall into sin. The idea of submission in marriage mirrors the concept of two becoming one flesh and the mutual sharing of each other's bodies. This union involves trust and caring for one another's physical and emotional well-being.

It is similar to placing oneself under the authority and protection of God. This principle provides a framework for marriage, and each person's circumstances must be taken into account.

In this passage, the husband is addressed first. Elsewhere in Scripture, husbands are called to love their wives as Christ loved the Church—with sacrificial, unconditional love. When the husband sets the tone for the relationship with love and understanding, it inspires the wife to respond with reciprocal love and trust.

True biblical submission to God is rooted in love, trust, and humility. It involves actively surrendering one's will to God's guidance and aligning one's life with His purposes, all while recognizing and affirming one's inherent value, dignity, and worth as a beloved child of God. Biblical submission to a husband and to other Christians is grounded in love, mutual respect as heirs of grace, and the recognition of our interconnectedness as members of the body of Christ. As the bride of Christ, we are a reflection of our Husband, Jesus. Just as Jesus submitted to the Father's will out of love and obedience, women are called to submit to God's loving authority, knowing that His plans are for their welfare and not for harm. **Jeremiah 29:11**

Some equate submission with being passive and silent. However, surrender to God is about being completely vulnerable and open, engaging with Him in a deeply personal and intimate relationship. Jesus is our Husband. We are His bride. Our prayers come from an open heart, with faith that we are loved, heard, and that our needs and feelings matter to Him. In reading His Word, we listen to His response and actively surrender our will to His divine plan, trusting in His wisdom and guidance. It is a dynamic relationship with God, where communication and openness are key.

Mutual submission within marriage reflects a reciprocal relationship grounded in love, grace, and trust—benefiting both partners, not one-sided toward the husband. While God calls us to submit to His will, He also promises to guide, protect, and provide for His children. God invites women to participate in His redemptive work in the world, to live out the reality of Christ in us, and to share His love and our testimony. Our relationship with Christ is our highest relationship—and also a model for what marriage is meant to be. There is no oppression or restriction of emotions or needs in Him, but rather liberation and freedom to be our true selves.

Submission to God encompasses every aspect of life by allowing His truth to permeate every area—including relationships, careers, and personal development; surrendering our whole selves to God's transformative power.

Ephesians 5:21-33 "*Submitting to one another out of reverence for Christ. Wives, submit to your own husbands, as to the Lord. For the husband is the head of the wife even as Christ is the head of the church, his body, and is himself its Savior. Now as the church submits to Christ, so also wives should submit in everything to their husbands. Husbands, love your wives, as Christ loved the church and gave himself up for her, that he might sanctify her, having cleansed her by the washing of water with the word...*" **Verse 21** begins with the exhortation to "*submit to one another out of reverence for Christ,*" introducing the principle of mutual submission, care, and equality within marriage. Husbands and wives are called to honor and serve one another in the unity of Christ, recognizing each other's inherent worth and dignity as individuals created in the image of God. The specific roles are given to show the purpose God has for marriage. It is a call for both husbands and wives to submit to Christ first. Wives are called to willingly yield to their husbands' leadership with respect, as to Christ. Husbands are called to love their wives as Christ loves the church—the body of Christ.

A Christian marriage parallels the union that exists spiritually between Christ and His bride, the body of Christ. We are all the bride of Christ. The husband is to teach by word and example in spiritual leadership, as both spouses go through the sanctification process to become more holy together, with a shared love and reverence for Christ. It was never meant to be a directive for unilateral authority or dominance.

Just as Christ is one with the Father, wives are equal to their husbands and are one with them. A wife voluntarily places herself under her husband's authority as she does to Christ. In marriage, husbands and wives have different roles, but their response to God's directives arises from their own submission to Christ first and foremost, and from the love they have been shown. Paul's emphasis for husbands is to love self-sacrificially, as Christ loves His bride. This kind of love is willing to lay down one's life to protect and support her. Paul stresses the love a husband must have for his wife, not his authority over her.

God knows the differences between women and men and the ways that can enhance the marriage relationship. Women respond to being shown love and affection. Men respond best when they are respected. However, both partners need love and respect from each other. Becoming one flesh signifies a bond, a sense of security and belonging within the union of marriage—both to each other and to God as one, for a total of three in unity.

1 Peter 3:7 "*Husbands, live with your wives in an understanding way, showing honor to the woman as the weaker vessel, since they are heirs with you of the grace of life, so that your prayers may not be hindered.*" Husbands are told to be understanding with their wives. This means recognizing and respecting their wives' vulnerabilities and treating them with dignity. Husbands are to cherish and honor their wives or their or their prayers may be hindered (**1 Peter 3:7**). Women, on average, are physically weaker and more emotional, which can lead to certain challenges or susceptibilitites. This does not diminish their worth

116

or value in any way. By reminding men that their wives are heirs with them, Scripture emphasizes again their equal standing before God.

Submission is a voluntary surrender to God's will—placing oneself under His authority, protection, and guidance—recognizing that God's purposes are higher and greater than her own desires, plans, and dreams for her life. Through prayer, studying Scripture, and listening to the prompting of the Holy Spirit, she can align with God's values and Kingdom principles as outlined in the Bible.

Let's take a look at the meaning of biblical submission:

James 4:7 – *"Submit yourselves therefore to God. Resist the devil, and he will flee from you."* The word *"submit"* in this verse comes from the Greek hypotagete, which carries the idea of willingly placing oneself under the authority or control of another. In Hebrew, the concept of submission is deeply rooted in the word shâ'âh, meaning to bow down, to humble oneself, or to surrender. This in no way removes a person's choice or free will, as may occur in some human relationships.

Submission is similar to voluntarily boarding a ship at sea. We trust the captain to navigate treacherous waters, knowing he is skilled, knowledgeable, and committed to our safety. As women, we are passengers who entrust our lives to God, voluntarily placing ourselves under His authority for safety and guidance—out of love, trust, and reverence. His leadership is characterized by wisdom, compassion, and unconditional love. He understands our struggles and guides us with perfect care. Under His care, we are safe, knowing He will navigate us away from spiritual danger and lead us to our destination.

He invites us into relationship—to come boldly to the helm in faith and obedience. With Jesus as our anchor and lighthouse, we sail through life's storms with confidence, surrendering our will to His divine guidance. In contrast to oppressive views of submission that promote control and fear, this voluntary act fosters intimacy. We experience the freedom Jesus came to give us—spiritual growth and fulfillment. There is much He wants to do in us and through us.

The Bible provides clear guidance on submission and equality that helps us understand God's design:

Genesis 1:27 – *"So God created man in His own image, in the image of God He created him; male and female He created them."* This verse affirms the equality of men and women, as both are created in the image of God. It emphasizes that both genders share the same divine image and are therefore inherently equal in value, dignity, and worth.

Galatians 3:28 – *"There is neither Jew nor Greek, there is neither slave nor free, there is no male and female, for you are all one in Christ Jesus."* This verse underscores the equality of all believers in Christ—regardless of gender, social status, or ethnicity—challenging any notion of hierarchy in submission to a husband based on these factors.

Matthew 20:25-28 *"But Jesus called them to him and said, 'You know that the rulers of the Gentiles lord it over them, and their great ones exercise authority over them. It shall* *not be so among you. But whoever would be great among you must be your servant, and whoever would be first among you must be your slave, even as the Son of Man came not to be served but to serve, and to give his life as a ransom for many."*

These verses reveal the heart of true submission—and challenge any notion of leadership based on dominance and control. Jesus Christ modeled servant leadership and demonstrated perfect submission to God the Father. Submission was never designed as a weapon of oppression, but as a voluntary act of love and trust within the protective covering of God's divine order.

For the single woman, submission to God becomes a shield of protection and guidance as she navigates life's journey. For the married woman, submission functions within the context of mutual surrender, where both husband and wife first submit to God, then to one another out of reverence for Christ. The husband's call to sacrificial love mirrors Christ's willingness to lay down His life—the ultimate act of service, not domination. The wife's voluntary submission is not a diminishment of her worth, but a recognition of God's ordained harmony within the marital relationship.

In both cases, submission finds its purest expression when freely given—never coerced or demanded. Just as Christ does not force our surrender but invites our willing hearts, submission in human relationships must reflect that same spirit of freedom and dignity.

My hope and prayer is that this section brings a deeper understanding of God's design for submission—not as a tool for control, but as a sacred invitation into deeper intimacy with Him and with a spouse. I pray that God replaces disappointment with His all-sufficient grace, and that emptiness is filled with His unconditional love. For the married, may you experience deeper connection with your spouse in unity and mutual respect. For all women—single, married, divorced, or separated—may you encounter Jesus, the Soul Healer, in a transformative way. May His touch mend wounds from misinterpretation, control, or abuse, and may His light guide your path forward. May you discover deeper intimacy with the Captain of your soul and a fresh revelation of your worth as His daughter.

As you embrace this journey, may you walk in God's purpose for you, shining as a beacon of His love in a world longing for redemption. There is hope. His name is Jesus. This book is a space for healing, growth, and empowerment—equipping women like you to embrace your God-given purpose with newfound confidence and clarity so you can live out your divine calling fully equipped and ready.

LOVE

At the heart of the Kingdom of God is the principle of love. Jesus taught in **Mark 12:30–31** that *"loving God with all our heart, soul, mind, and strength, and loving our neighbor as ourselves"* summarizes all the commandments. God's character is love. **1 John 4:8** says, *"Anyone who does not love does not know God, because God is love."*

Believers are called to embody God's unconditional love in their interactions. Jesus' life, teachings, and sacrifice exemplified perfect love and obedience to God's will. God's deep, unconditional love is the ultimate expression of His nature and the motivating force behind the salvation offered through Jesus. **John 3:16** states, *"For God so loved the world that He gave His only begotten Son, that whoever believes in Him will not perish but have everlasting life."* Jesus paid the ultimate sacrifice, enduring great pain to secure eternal life for us. God's love built a bridge through Jesus, bringing us into relationship with our Heavenly Father. This love cost Him His Son's life, revealing our worth and value.

Knowing we are securely and deeply loved by God, we are motivated to extend that love to others—living out our faith and seeing each soul through the compassionate eyes of Christ. We love God and our neighbors not out of obligation, but from gratitude and thankfulness, mirroring the love we have received.

As women, our nurturing spirit and empathy uniquely position us to radiate God's boundless love. This Kingdom principle compels us to show love through comforting words, a listening ear, or acts of kindness that affirm and uplift others. By fully embracing this principle, we radiate Christ's love, creating ripples of grace far beyond our immediate circles.

Application: How can I cultivate a deeper love for God and show the love of Jesus to others in word and deed—even those who may be difficult to love? What steps can I take to demonstrate God's love in my relationships and interactions?

Prayer
Lord, fill my heart with Your love, that I may see others as You see them and extend Your grace in every interaction. In Jesus' name, Amen.

JUSTICE

The Kingdom of God upholds justice and righteousness—it is the very nature of God. **Psalm 7:11** says that He is a *"righteous Judge"* and **Psalm 11:7** *"For the Lord is righteous, He loves justice; His countenance beholds the upright."* Believers are called to seek justice. **Micah 6:8** declares, *"He has told you, O man, what is good; and what does the Lord require of you but to do justice, and to love kindness, and to walk humbly with your God?"* This includes advocating for the marginalized and oppressed—from the unborn to the elderly—reflecting the value and dignity God places on all human life as people created in His image. We echo God's heart by standing against wrongdoing, actively working to bring about change—speaking up for those who cannot speak for themselves, defending the rights of the poor and needy. This can be expressed through acts of feeding the homeless, caring for orphans and widows, advocating against abortion, supporting adoption and foster care, combating sex trafficking, opposing euthanasia, and generously sharing resources and time. We are called to engage in spiritual warfare, interceding in prayer for justice to prevail. Justice in the Kingdom is not merely legal fairness—but rooted in God's righteousness, mercy, and truth. **Isaiah 1:17** urges us to *"learn to do good; seek justice, correct oppression; bring justice to the fatherless, plead the widow's cause."* When we pursue justice, we reflect God's heart and help bring restoration to a broken world. This sacred duty is not optional for believers; it is an extension of living out the gospel in action.

Reflection: How can I advocate for justice in my community or support efforts that promote equity and support for the marginalized and oppressed?

What steps can I take to advocate for fairness and justice in my personal life or community?

Prayer - Heavenly Father, guide me in Your wisdom to advocate for justice and righteousness in my actions and words. In Jesus' name. Amen

HUMILITY

Humility is a key principle in the Kingdom of God. Jesus taught that *"those who humble themselves will be exalted,"* and *"those who exalt themselves will be humbled"* (**Luke 14:11**). Believers are called to imitate Christ's humility in their attitudes and actions. **Proverbs 16:18** warns, *"Pride goes before destruction, and a haughty spirit before a fall."* **James 4:6** reminds us, *"God opposes the proud but gives grace to the humble."*

By embracing a humble heart, we mirror Christ's own humility and open ourselves to God's guidance, allowing His purpose for our lives to unfold gracefully—unimpeded by pride or vanity. Jesus modeled humility perfectly; despite His divinity, He knelt to wash the feet of His disciples. He invites us to serve rather than be served, to place others' needs above our own, and to acknowledge our need for Him. We are not to rely on our own strength, but to live in full dependence on Him.

Humility is not weakness—it is strength under control, rooted in a proper view of ourselves in light of who God is. **Philippians 2:3-5** teaches, *"Do nothing from selfish ambition or conceit, but in humility count others more significant than yourselves... Have this mind among yourselves, which is yours in Christ Jesus."* True humility recognizes that every good thing we have is a gift from God, and it enables us to lift others up, build unity, and walk in obedience. As we cultivate humility, we reflect the heart of Christ and become vessels through which God's grace and love flow to others.

Reflection: Are there areas where pride or arrogance may be hindering your ability to serve others effectively? What steps can you take to exhibit greater humility in your thoughts, words or actions?

Prayer - God, teach me humility, that I may serve You and others selflessly, recognizing Your hand in all my achievements. In Jesus' name. Amen

FORGIVENESS

Forgiveness is pivotal in the Kingdom of God. Jesus taught that we are to extend grace and forgiveness to others as we have been forgiven by God, mirroring the infinite mercy of God and liberating hearts from resentment and bitterness. *"For if you forgive others their trespasses, your heavenly Father will also forgive you, but if you do not forgive others their trespasses, neither will your Father forgive your trespasses"* (**Matthew 6:14–15**). This is the path that leads to peace and reconciliation. By forgiving, we display the infinite mercy we have received from Christ, paving the way for healing and restoration in our lives. This act is especially powerful for those who have endured trauma and pain, opening doors to new beginnings and, at times, restoration in relationships.

Forgiveness is not about excusing injustice or denying the pain we've experienced—it is a deliberate act of surrendering our right to retaliate and entrusting justice to God. **Romans 12:19** reminds us, *"Beloved, never avenge yourselves, but leave it to the wrath of God, for it is written, 'Vengeance is mine, I will repay, says the Lord.'"* When we forgive, we are not saying the offense was acceptable; rather, we are choosing to walk in obedience and freedom; refusing to be chained to the person who harmed us or the wounds of the past. By choosing forgiveness we give their life over to Jesus to judge and deal with. Forgiveness brings us into alignment with God's heart, softens us to His healing touch, and frees us to love more fully.

Reflection: Is there anyone you need to forgive or seek forgiveness from? What steps can I take to foster a spirit of forgiveness, release hurts, and extend grace as a reflection of the forgiveness you have received from God?

Prayer - Lord, grant me the strength to feel my angry emotions from the wounds inflicted by others and to forgive them as You have forgiven me. Help me to let go of resentment and bitterness. I give You any judgment for what they have done to harm me or others. I thank You for freeing my heart from any unforgiveness. In Jesus' name. Amen

SERVANTHOOD

Jesus exemplified that true greatness in the Kingdom of God is achieved through heartfelt service to others by modeling servant leadership. Instead of seeking positions of authority or power as the Gentiles did, He taught us to serve one another with humility and selflessness. **Mark 10:43–45** declares, *"But whoever would be great among you must be your servant, and whoever would be first among you must be slave of all. For even the Son of Man came not to be served but to serve, and to give his life as a ransom for many."*

By pointing to His own life, Jesus revealed that true greatness is found in humble service and sacrificial love for others. Embracing servanthood not only transforms our daily interactions but also propels us toward a life rich with purpose and profound influence. Biblical servanthood in the Kingdom of God flips the world's definition of greatness on its head. We follow Jesus' example by caring for our families, supporting our communities, and volunteering our talents in the Body of Christ. In serving the least among us, we serve Christ Himself (**Matthew 25:40**), demonstrating the gospel in tangible ways and inviting others to experience God's love.

Reflection: In what ways can I serve within my community, church or family without expecting anything in return? What steps can I take using the talents God has given me—to serve others selflessly?

Prayer - Jesus, mold me into a servant like You, eager to uplift others and put their needs before my own. In Jesus' name. Amen

123

FAITH

Faith is the cornerstone of our spiritual journey and vital for navigating life's storms. It empowers us to trust in God's unchanging character, to hold firm to His promises, and to believe in the miraculous even when we cannot see His hand at work. Small yet steadfast acts of faith can catalyze monumental changes in our lives and in the world around us.

Jesus taught us about faith in **Matthew 17:20**: *"For truly, I say to you, if you have faith like a grain of mustard seed, you will say to this mountain, 'Move from here to there,' and it will move, and nothing will be impossible for you."* This mountain-moving faith enables us to face uncertainty with courage and determination. As we nurture our faith through prayer, study, and fellowship, we discover an inner strength that sustains us through every trial. Believers are called to trust in God's promises and rely on His power to accomplish His purposes.

Faith also binds us together as the Body of Christ. When we share testimonies of God's faithfulness, pray for one another, and encourage each other, our collective faith deepens. **Hebrews 10:24–25** urges us to *"consider how to stir up one another to love and good works"* and *"not to neglect meeting together"*. In community, our individual faith is strengthened, and we become living witnesses to God's grace.

Reflection: Are there areas in your life where fear or doubt is holding you back from fully trusting God's plan? What practical steps can you take today to walk by faith and not by sight?

Prayer - Heavenly Father, deepen my faith, that I may trust in Your promises and boldly step forward in Your plans. In Jesus' name. Amen

HOLINESS

We are called to a life of holiness, striving to honor God in all we do. **1 Peter 1:15–16** declares, *"But as He who called you is holy, you also be holy in all your conduct, since it is written, 'You shall be holy, for I am holy.'"* This pursuit is a daily commitment to purity and integrity that influences every intent of our heart and shapes our conduct. Holiness calls us to lives set apart for God—not merely moral purity, but embodying His love and grace in everything we do. It challenges us to examine our thoughts, words, and actions, ensuring they align with God's will. As women, our example of godliness can inspire others to seek a deeper relationship with Christ. Living a holy life also means offering ourselves fully to God's service. **Romans 12:1** urges us, *"Present your bodies as a living sacrifice, holy and acceptable to God, which is your spiritual worship."* By surrendering our ambitions, preferences, and time, we allow the Holy Spirit to transform us from the inside out. In practical terms, this may look like choosing integrity over convenience, speaking truth in love, or extending grace when it's undeserved. As we pursue holiness together, in community, prayer, and Scripture—we reflect God's character and become beacons of His light in a world that so desperately needs it.

Reflection: What areas of my life do I feel God is calling me to change in order to reflect His holiness, purity, and devotion? What steps can I take to avoid compromising my values and standards in a world that promotes secular ideals?

Prayer - Lord, sanctify me, that I may live a life pleasing to You, set apart and pure in thought, word, and deed. In Jesus' name. Amen

125

UNITY

Unity is the lifeline of the body of Christ, a living testament to God's love. We are called to live in peace, unity, and harmony as far as it depends upon us, strengthening our collective witness to the world. Jesus prayed for this oneness among His followers "*so that the world may believe*" (**John 17:20–23**). Divisions are to be avoided: "*I appeal to you, brothers, by the name of our Lord Jesus Christ, that all of you agree, and that there be no divisions among you, but that you be united in the same mind and the same judgment*" (**1 Corinthians 1:10**). Likewise, we are instructed to turn away from those who cause discord, for such behavior is contrary to the gospel (**Romans 16:17**).

As women, we can be bridge-builders of mutual respect by creating spaces that value diversity and encourage unity in faith and purpose. We discourage gossip by refusing to repeat rumors or engage in anything that devalues or divides believers—each of whom is deeply valued in God's eyes.

Furthermore, unity demands intentional effort and sacrifice. **Ephesians 4:3** exhorts us to "*make every effort to keep the unity of the Spirit through the bond of peace.*" This means listening with empathy, seeking reconciliation when conflict arises, and celebrating the diverse gifts God has given each member. When we prioritize the common good over personal preferences, we embody Christ's love and create a witness that draws others to Him.

Reflection: Are there conflicts or divisions you need to address with humility and grace? What steps can you take to promote unity and harmony within your family, church or community?

Prayer - Father, unify Your people that we may be one as You are One, with the faith that binds us, despite our differences to demonstrate the power of Your love. In Jesus' name. Amen

GENEROUSITY

Generosity is a characteristic of the Kingdom of God. The spirit of generosity mirrors the very heart of God. By giving freely—not only of our material possessions but of our time and talents—we reflect God's generous heart and display His character. Believers are called to give from the abundance their heavenly Father has provided. **James 1:17** reminds us, "*Every good gift and every perfect gift is from above, coming down from the Father of lights, with whom there is no variation or shadow due to change.*"

God blesses those who give cheerfully, for "*God loves a cheerful giver*" (**2 Corinthians 9:7**). This giving can take many forms: sharing resources, offering our time, extending love, exercising our talents, and providing spiritual mentoring—all flowing from what God has entrusted to us. The ripples of generosity build community, support the needy, spread joy, and transform lives. Generosity also flows from a heart of worship and gratitude, acknowledging that everything we have ultimately belongs to God (**Psalm 24:1**). In giving, we invest in eternal purposes and store up treasures in heaven, as Jesus taught (**Matthew 6:20**). **Acts 20:35** further encourages us with the words of Jesus: "*It is more blessed to give than to receive.*" God is able "*to make all grace abound to you, so that having all sufficiency in all things at all times, you may abound in every good work*" (**2 Corinthians 9:8**).

Reflection: Are there areas where you can sacrificially give to support those in need and share your resources as an act of worship and gratitude towards God? What steps can you take to be more generous with your resources, time and talents?

Prayer — God, open my hands and heart to give generously, reflecting Your generosity in every gift and action. Help me to give cheerfully and without holding back, from all that You give me. In Jesus' name. Amen

ETERNAL PERSPECTIVE

The Kingdom of God offers an eternal perspective that transcends earthly concerns. Believers are encouraged to *"set their minds on things above, where Christ is seated at the right hand of God"* (**Colossians 3:1–2**), not on earthly things, and to live with an eternal mindset instead of being consumed by the temporary. Living with an eternal perspective transforms how we view our lives and our world, compelling us to focus on long-term Kingdom impact rather than short-term gain.

By directing our thoughts toward heavenly realities, we are reminded of the eternal significance of our actions, words, and decisions. This shift in perspective helps us prioritize spiritual values over worldly pursuits and guides us to live according to God's will. Ultimately, an eternal perspective anchors our hearts in the unshakable truth of God's Word, allowing us to persevere through life's trials with peace and purpose. It invites us to fix our eyes not on what is seen, but on what is unseen, for *"what is seen is temporary, but what is unseen is eternal"* (**2 Corinthians 4:18**).

Adopting this mindset helps us shift our priorities, motivating us to invest in what truly matters: cultivating godly relationships, walking in righteousness, and sharing the gospel. It reminds us that souls matter deeply to God, and that our true citizenship is in heaven (**Philippians 3:20**). Every act of obedience, love, and faith becomes an offering that echoes in eternity. As we live with this eternal perspective, we step into our God-given purpose and prepare our hearts for the everlasting Kingdom.

Each of these principles intertwine to form a beautiful tapestry of Kingdom living, empowered by the guidance of the Holy Spirit—as we continue to grow and mature in our faith. Let us draw closer to the heart and character of God, seeking His transformative touch in every area of our lives, that we may become all He has created us to be and fulfill the unique calling He has placed within us.

Reflection: Which area of Kingdom living—faith, forgiveness, humility, service, holiness, generosity, or unity—is God inviting you to grow in right now?

Prayer— Gracious Father, we come before You with hearts full of gratitude. Thank You for carrying us through the storms and for the hope You give us in every season. Clothe us in humility as we submit to You. Fill us with Your love, and empower us to forgive, serve, give, love justice, and walk in holiness. Strengthen our faith to stand firm, keep our eyes fixed on eternity, and help us to live out our purpose on purpose with joy and boldness. Unite us in spirit and mission as we reflect Your Kingdom on earth. In Jesus' name, Amen.

CHAPTER 12

Spiritual Growth and Practices

PRAISE AND WORSHIP

Even if you are still discovering your specific purpose in life, know that the highest calling for every woman is to praise and worship God. This divine connection forms the foundation of your journey toward understanding your unique calling and living it with authenticity and passion.

Understanding the Distinction

There are very distinct differences between praise and worship that every woman seeking her purpose should understand:

Praise

- Acknowledges and appreciates God's actions, qualities, and achievements
- **Psalm 100:4** instructs us to "*Enter His gates with thanksgiving and His courts with praise*"
- Is expressed through singing, psalms, hymns, shouting, dance, and musical instruments and can be boisterous, joyful and uninhibited
- It focuses on what God has done - His characteristics, His deeds, creation, miracles, and blessings— and is closely intertwined with thanksgiving
- Can be a part of worship but is not the entirety of worship
- Jesus says that if people don't praise God, even the rocks will cry out

Worship

- Worship is a deeper, more profound act reserved exclusively for God
- It arises from the depths of our heart, the understanding of our mind, and the devotion of our soul
- Worship encompasses complete and sincere commitment to God's presence, will, and authority
- It focuses solely on who God is rather than just what He has done—His divine nature, holiness, omnipotence, omniscience, and omnipresence
- **John 4:24** emphasizes the need for heartfelt, authentic worship guided by the Holy Spirit
- Worship can take various forms including prayer, meditation, and sacrificial acts
- True worship is from the heart— a person can go through the motions without actual worship
- Worship is described in scripture as the act of bowing down, coupled with a revelation of God's presence
- The Father seeks those who will worship Him in Spirit and in truth

"I tell you," He replied, "if they keep quiet, the stones will cry out."

Luke 19:40

ELEMENTS OF WORSHIP

SURRENDER

Surrender is the act of giving up our own will and desires to follow God's will—trusting Him completely and letting go of control. True fulfillment comes from aligning with God's plan, demonstrating our trust, faith, and reliance on Him.

SINGING

A powerful way to express worship and praise is by vocalizing love and adoration for God through music. It glorifies God, uplifts the spirit, and draws others closer to Him, making our singing a testimony of faith and love.

ADORATION

Adoration is deep love and reverence for God—spending time in His presence, marveling at His greatness, and loving Him with all your heart. It deepens and strengthens our connection with God, fueling our life's purpose and passion.

TESTIMONY

Our testimony is a powerful form of worship, recounting how Jesus has transformed our lives. He turns trials into testimonies and messes into messages. By boldly sharing what Jesus has done in us and through us, we glorify God and show the world how He brings good from evil, inspiring hope and faith in others.

SERVICE

Service is worship in action—using our gifts to serve others and meet their needs, reflecting God's love through our deeds. It honors God and makes His love tangible through selfless actions, following Jesus' example of service. **Matthew 20:28**

OBEDIENCE

Obedience is following God's commands and aligning our actions with His will. It is a profound form of worship that honors God's instructions and makes us beacons of His light and truth. Jesus emphasized, *"If you love me, keep my commands"* **John 14:15**

MEDITATION ON SCRIPTURE

Meditation on Scripture involves reflecting deeply on God's Word to understand and apply it in our lives. Regular meditation treasures His word in our hearts, growing in wisdom and faith, enabling us to live out our purpose with clarity and conviction **Psalm 1:1-2**

FELLOWSHIP

Fellowship is gathering with other believers to worship, encourage, and support one another in faith. Community strengthens relationships, provides mutual support, and fosters unity and collective worship, as exemplified by the early Christians **Acts 2:42-47**

132

PRAISE BIBLE VERSES

PSALM 150:1-6

"Praise the Lord! Praise God in His sanctuary; praise Him in His mighty heavens! Praise Him for His mighty deeds; praise Him according to His excellent greatness! Praise Him with trumpet sound; praise Him with lute and harp! Praise Him with tambourine and dance; praise Him with strings and pipe! Praise Him with sounding cymbals; praise Him with loud clashing cymbals! Let everything that has breath praise the Lord! Praise the Lord!"

PSALM 95:1-6

"Oh come, let us sing to the Lord; let us make a joyful noise to the rock of our salvation! Let us come into His presence with thanksgiving; let us make a joyful noise to Him with songs of praise! For the Lord is a great God, and a great King above all gods. In His hand are the depths of the earth; the heights of the mountains are His also. The sea is His, for He made it, and His hands formed the dry land. Oh come, let us worship and bow down; let us kneel before the Lord, our Maker!"

PSALM 96:1-4

"Oh sing to the Lord a new song; sing to the Lord, all the earth! Sing to the Lord, bless His name; tell of His salvation from day to day. Declare His glory among the nations, His marvelous works among all the peoples! For great is the Lord, and greatly to be praised; He is to be feared above all gods."

PSALM 100:1-5

"Make a joyful noise to the Lord, all the earth! Serve the Lord with gladness! Come into His presence with singing! Know that the Lord, He is God! It is He who made us, and we are His; we are His people, and the sheep of His pasture. Enter His gates with thanksgiving, and His courts with praise! Give thanks to Him; bless His name! For the Lord is good; His steadfast love endures forever, and His faithfulness to all generations."

PSALM 150:6

"Let everything that has breath praise the Lord! Praise the Lord!"

WORSHIP BIBLE VERSES

JOHN 4:23-24

"But the hour is coming, and is now here, when the true worshipers will worship the Father in spirit and truth, for the Father is seeking such people to worship Him. God is spirit, and those who worship Him must worship in spirit and truth."

PSALM 100:2

"Worship the Lord with gladness; come before Him with joyful songs."

EXODUS 20:3-5

"You shall have no other gods before me. You shall not make for yourself a carved image, or any likeness of anything that is in heaven above, or that is in the earth beneath, or that is in the water under the earth. You shall not bow down to them or serve them, for I the Lord your God am a jealous God,"

MATTHEW 4:10

"Then Jesus said to him, 'Be gone, Satan! For it is written, "You shall worship the Lord your God and Him only shall you serve."'"

ROMANS 12:1

"I appeal to you therefore, brothers, by the mercies of God, to present your bodies as a living sacrifice, holy and acceptable to God, which is your spiritual worship."

REVELATION 22:8-9

"I, John, am the one who heard and saw these things. And when I heard and saw them, I fell down to worship at the feet of the angel who showed them to me, but he said to me, 'You must not do that! I am a fellow servant with you and your brothers the prophets, and with those who keep the words of this book. Worship God.'"

PSALM 29:2

"Ascribe to the Lord the glory due His name; worship the Lord in the splendor of holiness."

HEBREWS 12:28-29

"Therefore let us be grateful for receiving a kingdom that cannot be shaken, and thus let us offer to God acceptable worship, with reverence and awe, for our God is a consuming fire."

PRAYER

As a daughter of God, a woman of purpose values prayer whether she is a teacher, spiritual leader, mentor or disciple. Prayer is a direct line of communication with God—a powerful and essential practice in discovering and fulfilling our purpose. It involves drawing close to His heart, speaking to Him, listening for His guidance, and interceding for others. A woman's prayers are vital to daily worship, seeking God's wisdom and direction, aligning her heart with His, and interceding for those around her to fulfill the specific role God has given her.

God promises to hear His people's prayers. **1 John 5:14-15** says, *"And this is the confidence that we have toward him, that if we ask anything according to His will he hears us. And if we know that He hears us in whatever we ask, we know that we have the requests that we have asked of Him."* This assurance encourages us to approach God confidently.

Prayer strengthens our connection with God. Like any relationship, communication and intimacy are essential for closeness. Through communicating with Him, we seek wisdom and direction for our lives (**James 1:5**), find comfort and peace in times of trouble by casting our anxiety upon the Lord (**Philippians 4:6–7**), and experience His promise to draw near to us when we draw near to Him (**James 4:8**).

Prayer is integral to discovering and fulfilling the divine calling God has for your life. Through prayer we seek Him to provide clarity, direction, wisdom, strength and inspiration to pursue God's unique path for us with confidence. We gain spiritual growth and maturity as we remain grounded in faith and seek His guidance to navigate life's challenges. God invites us to bring our requests to Him. **James 4:2-3** reminds us that sometimes *"we have not because we do not ask"* or *"we do not receive because we ask wrongly, to spend on our passions."*

We can never go wrong by asking for God's will in our lives, as He is a good Father. **Matthew 7:11** says, *"If you then, who are evil, know how to give good gifts to your children, how much more will your Father who is in heaven give good things to those who ask Him!"* God's wisdom far surpasses our own, and He understands the long-term impact of our requests. Sometimes, He withholds certain things for our benefit, teaching us to trust in His perfect plan.

TYPES OF PRAYER

ADORATION

Adoration is the act of praising God for who He is—His majesty and His attributes. It involves recognizing God's infinite greatness and expressing deep love and reverence for Him. **Psalm 145:3** says, *"Great is the Lord, and greatly to be praised, and His greatness is unsearchable."* Through adoration, we acknowledge God's holiness, power, and mercy, filling our hearts with awe and gratitude for His presence.

CONFESSION

Confession involves acknowledging and repenting of sin, seeking God's forgiveness. It is essential for maintaining a healthy relationship with God, allowing us to come clean before Him and receive His mercy. **1 John 1:9** assures us, *"If we confess our sins, He is faithful and just to forgive us our sins and to cleanse us from all unrighteousness."* Through confession, we experience the cleansing power of God's forgiveness and are restored to right standing with Him.

THANKSGIVING

Thanksgiving is the expression of gratitude for God's blessings and answered prayers. It is a vital aspect of prayer, reminding us to recognize and appreciate God's goodness. **Philippians 4:6** encourages us, *"Do not be anxious about anything, but in everything by prayer and supplication with thanksgiving let your requests be made known to God."* Through thanksgiving, we cultivate a heart of gratitude, acknowledging God's provision and faithfulness.

SUPPLICATION

Supplication is the presentation of our needs and requests to God, asking for His intervention. It is an act of humbly coming before God, trusting Him to provide for our needs and the needs of others. **Ephesians 6:18** instructs us to *"pray at all times in the Spirit, with all prayer and supplication."* Through supplication, we demonstrate our dependence on God and our belief in His power to work in our lives and situations.

Intercession

Intercession is praying on behalf of others in need out of love and concern, asking God to intervene in their lives. It's standing in the gap, lifting their needs before God. **1 Timothy 2:1** urges, *"First of all, then, I urge that supplications, prayers, intercessions, and thanksgivings be made for all people."* Through intercession, we participate in God's blessings and the healing of others, and show our trust in God's ability to act.

Meditation

Meditation involves reflecting on God's Word and listening for His voice. It's a practice of focusing on Scripture, allowing God's truths to penetrate our hearts and renew our minds. **Psalm 19:14** expresses this beautifully: *"Let the words of my mouth and the meditation of my heart be acceptable in your sight, O Lord, my rock and my redeemer."* Through meditation, we deepen our understanding of God's Word, grow in spiritual wisdom, and align our thoughts with His will.

Lament

Lament prayers express sorrow, grief, or regret; often seeking God's comfort and intervention—acknowledging the reality of suffering and pain while appealing to God for His presence and help in distress. Many Psalms are prayers where the psalmist pours out heartache and anguish to God. **Psalm 22:1:** *"My God, my God, why have You forsaken me? Why are You so far from saving me, from the words of my groaning?"* Through lamenting we bring our deepest pain and struggles to God, finding solace and hope in His presence, affirming trust in God's faithfulness and compassion.

Warfare

Warfare prayers are a type of intercession focusing on spiritual battles, asking for God's intervention against evil forces. They recognize the reality of spiritual opposition, equip us to engage in spiritual warfare as we recognize the authority and power every believer possesses in the powerful name of Jesus Christ. They empower believers to stand firm against spiritual attacks, interceding for God's powerful protection and victory in their lives and the lives of others. **Ephesians 6:10-12** outlines the spiritual battle and the necessity of relying on God's strength: *"Finally, be strong in the Lord and in the strength of His might. Put on the whole armor of God, that you may be able to stand against the schemes of the devil.*

Giving thanks always and for everything to God the Father in the name of our Lord Jesus Christ.
~Ephesians 5:20

THANKFULNESS

Thankfulness is a foundational aspect of our faith journey as women of purpose; a practice deeply rooted in appreciating and recognizing God's goodness in our lives. It is more than mere politeness or acknowledging favor; it is a heart posture of gratitude that acknowledges God's sovereignty, protection, provision, grace, and love. Cultivating gratefulness reminds us of His abundant blessings. Every good gift we receive, whether tangible or intangible, reflects God's love and generosity.

Thankfulness humbles us to recognize that everything we have comes from God. By expressing gratitude, we develop a heart of contentment and trust in His faithfulness and goodness. It shifts our focus from self-centeredness to acknowledging God as the ultimate source of all blessings. In humility, we accept our dependence on Him and surrender our plans and desires in exchange for His.

Gratitude is a spiritual discipline that deepens our relationship with God. As we express thankfulness, we draw closer to Him and align our hearts with His, leading us to desire what He desires. It opens the door to communion with God, inviting His presence into our lives. Gratitude guards against complacency and entitlement by reminding us of the privilege of knowing and serving Him. It redirects our perspective from what we lack to appreciating what we have, cultivating generosity and stewardship—using our blessings to bless others.

Thankfulness fosters joy and contentment regardless of circumstances. When we focus on blessings rather than challenges, we celebrate God's goodness and experience peace and fulfillment. It is our response to God's love and grace through Jesus Christ. His sacrifice reveals the depth of God's love and prompts us to live with gratitude and a spirit open to His will and guidance.

For women seeking purpose, thankfulness nurtures receptiveness to God's direction. Gratitude for opportunities leads to a deeper awareness of His faithfulness, empowering us to step boldly into our calling, grounded in the truth of His promises. Let us cultivate thankfulness and celebrate God's goodness in every aspect of our lives every day of our lives.

WHAT I'M THANKFUL FOR

CHAPTER 13

Spiritual Warfare

SPIRITUAL WARFARE

From the beginning, God intended humanity to rule and reign with Him by giving them dominion over the earth's creatures (**Genesis 1:26**), instructing them to *"be fruitful and multiply, fill the earth and subdue it"* (**Genesis 1:28**). God established humans as stewards of creation for His intended purposes. However, the fall of man through Adam and Eve's disobedience introduced sin, death, and disorder into the world. As a result, humanity was separated from God, and Satan became *"the prince of the power of the air"* (**Ephesians 2:2**) and is referred to as *"the god of this world"* (**2 Corinthians 4:4**), indicating that he holds a measure of authority and influence over the earthly realm.

This influence is manifested through deception, temptation, and the propagation of evil, all aimed at undermining God's purposes and leading people away from Him. However, Jesus Christ came to redeem creation, triumphing over Satan and his forces. As **Colossians 2:15** explains, Jesus *"disarmed the rulers and authorities and put them to open shame, by triumphing over them in Him."* This victory means that while Satan can still influence and tempt, he no longer holds dominion over believers who are in Christ.

Through His triumph on the cross, Jesus granted us authority over all the power of the enemy—a power specifically rooted in our identity in Christ and the victory He secured over the forces of darkness. As joint heirs with Christ, we are called to stand firm against the enemy's schemes, to be more than conquerors, and to walk in the victory that He has already secured as overcomers because He overcame the world.

As women of purpose, we must recognize the reality of this spiritual conflict. The apostle Paul reminds us in **Ephesians 6:12** that *"we do not wrestle against flesh and blood, but against the rulers, against the authorities, against the cosmic powers over this present darkness, against the spiritual forces of evil in the heavenly places."* This means our struggles often have spiritual dimensions that require spiritual weapons. When we face opposition in fulfilling our God-given purpose, we must discern whether we are encountering natural obstacles or spiritual resistance.

Jesus demonstrated this authority when He gave His disciples power over unclean spirits, commanding them to *"heal the sick, raise the dead, cleanse lepers, cast out demons"* (**Matthew 10:8**). Later, He promised that believers would do *"even greater works"* (**John 14:12**). This authority is not reserved for a select few but for all who are in Christ.

As women of purpose, we can confidently exercise this God-given authority through prayer, speaking God's Word, and standing in our identity as daughters of the Most High God. When we understand who we are in Christ and the victory He has already won, we can face spiritual battles not from a position of fear, but from a position of triumph—knowing that *"He who is in you is greater than he who is in the world"* (**1 John 4:4**).

Satan's Strategies Against Believers

DECEPTION

Satan, known as the *"father of lies"* (**John 8:44**), uses deception to cause believers to doubt their identity in Christ and the authority they possess. His ultimate goal is to distort God's truth and lead them off the path of righteousness. By sowing seeds of doubt, fear, lies, and confusion, he aims to weaken believers' confidence in their faith and purpose. The antidote is to stand firm on God's Word, renew the mind through Scripture, rely on the Holy Spirit for discernment and strength, and boldly use the powerful name of Jesus.

ACCUSATION

Another key tactic of Satan is accusation. Referred to as *"the accuser of the brethren"* (**Revelation 12:10**), he constantly reminds believers of past sins, failures, and shortcomings to burden them with guilt and shame. By turning their focus to past mistakes, he attempts to make them forget the forgiveness and grace they have received in Christ. If successful, he can hinder their spiritual growth. Believers combat this by embracing the truth that Jesus has removed their shame, approaching God instead of hiding, affirming their identity in Christ, and resting in the assurance that *"there is now no condemnation for those who are in Christ Jesus"* (**Romans 8:1**).

FEAR

Fear is a strategy Satan uses to paralyze believers. He uses fear to cause them to question their ability and worthiness to fulfill their purpose. By magnifying fears of failure or harm, he works to keep believers from stepping into the fullness of God's plan for their lives. When Christians are afraid to step out in faith, confront spiritual battles, or take Kingdom-focused risks, they become stagnant and ineffective in fulfilling their God-given purpose. Fear may manifest as anxiety about the future, fear of harm, or a lack of confidence. Believers are exhorted to trust in God's provision and promises, stepping forward in faith even when fear is present, knowing that *"God has not given us a spirit of fear but of power, love, and a sound mind"* (**2 Timothy 1:7**).

DIVISION AND DISUNITY

Satan targets the unity of the Church by promoting division and strife among believers, aiming to weaken its strength and hinder its mission. Unity is essential for the body of Christ to fulfill its purpose. A divided Church loses its effectiveness and undermines its witness to the world. By sowing discord and conflict, Satan seeks to create factions that disrupt the Church's collective impact. **James 3:16** warns, *"For where you have envy and selfish ambition, there you find disorder and every evil practice."* To protect against this, believers must seek reconciliation, extend forgiveness, and prioritize love and humility —*"eager to maintain the unity of the Spirit in the bond of peace"* (**Ephesians 4:3**).

TEMPTATION AND SIN

After salvation, Satan continues to tempt believers, attempting to lure them back into sinful behaviors and patterns in an effort to weaken their spiritual growth and effectiveness. As shown in **Matthew 4:1-11**, Satan tempted Jesus in the wilderness, revealing how he seeks to undermine believers by appealing to their fleshly desires and human weaknesses, especially when they are vulnerable. This ongoing struggle with temptation requires believers to remain vigilant, relying on the power of Christ to resist and overcome such temptations. Scripture assures us that God provides a way of escape: "*No temptation has overtaken you except what is common to mankind. And God is faithful; He will not let you be tempted beyond what you can bear. But when you are tempted, He will also provide a way out so that you can endure it*" (**1 Corinthians 10:13**).

DISTRACTION AND WORLDLINESS

By enticing believers with worldly pleasures and distractions, Satan attempts to divert their focus from their devotion to God and their purpose to focus on the things of this world. This tactic causes believers to lose sight of their spiritual mission and goals. The allure of temporary, earthly pleasures and desires can lead to a loss of spiritual effectiveness. Believers must remain focused on eternal values and "*seek first the Kingdom of God*" (**Matthew 6:33**) to resist these distractions. John warns, "*Do not love the world or anything in the world. If anyone loves the world, the love for the Father is not in them*" (**1 John 2:15**).

ISOLATION AND VULNERABILITY

Satan attempts to isolate believers from the community of faith, making them more susceptible to discouragement and sin. **1 Peter 5:8** – "*Be sober-minded; be watchful. Your adversary the devil prowls around like a roaring lion, seeking someone to devour.*" Isolation weakens one's spiritual state and increases vulnerability to attacks intended to defeat them. This diminished accountability enhances the propensity to sin. Believers should actively engage with their faith community for support, prayer, and encouragement and participate in Bible studies to reinforce their spiritual resilience and health. We must build each other up and link our shields of faith together with other believers.

MISINTERPRETATION OF SCRIPTURE

Satan distorts and twists God's Word. By misquoting or taking Scripture out of context, he seeks to confuse believers leading them away from the truth into false doctrines and more pleasing theologies. Many Christians are deconstructing biblical truths, adopting progressive beliefs, and reshaping Scripture to align with modern desires and cultural norms. We must be diligent in studying and understanding the Bible to correctly interpret and apply God's Word. When we approach Scripture with humility and seek the guidance of the Holy Spirit, we can guard against deception and remain grounded in truth.

PRIDE AND SELF-RELIANCE

Satan fosters pride and self-reliance by tempting believers to depend on their own strength rather than trusting in God. This strategy was evident in the Garden of Eden when he enticed Eve with the promise that she could *"be like God"* (**Genesis 3:5**). Today, he continues to lure believers into relying on their own wisdom and abilities. Pride opens the door to deception and further sin. Proverbs **16:18** warns, *"Pride goes before destruction, a haughty spirit before a fall."* This makes humility and dependence on God essential (**Proverbs 3:5–6**). Satan understands that pride positions us in opposition to God, as *"God opposes the proud but gives grace to the humble"* (**James 4:6**). His goal is to blind us to our need for God, tempting us to declare, *"I have no need"* (**Revelation 3:17**), forgetting that *"apart from Christ, we can do nothing"* (**John 15:5**).

DESTRUCTION OF FAITH

Satan's ultimate goal is to destroy the faith of believers. Jesus described his mission clearly: *"The thief comes only to steal and kill and destroy"* (**John 10:10**). By undermining believers' faith and severing their connection to Christ—their true source of strength—Satan aims to make them ineffective in their walk and witness. But Jesus offers the antidote: *"I came that they may have life and have it abundantly"* (**John 10:10**). Believers are exhorted to *"be sober-minded; be watchful"* (**1 Peter 5:8**), for Satan targets faith because it is *"the victory that has overcome the world"* (**1 John 5:4**). Without faith, *"it is impossible to please God"* (**Hebrews 11:6**). Through trials and tribulations, he seeks to shake that foundation, which is why Peter urges, *"Resist him, firm in your faith"* (**1 Peter 5:9**).

SELF-PROTECTION

In the physical realm, people take precautions to protect themselves—installing security systems or keeping weapons for defense. These are practical responses to physical threats. Spiritually, however, Satan deceives believers into relying on their own protective measures rather than depending on God. He wants us to believe that our efforts are more effective than God's provision, drawing us into a mindset of self-reliance. Satan's strategy is to shift our trust away from God's covering, tempting us to take control and protect ourselves in our own strength. He tries to divert your trust from divine protection, causing you to neglect the spiritual armor God provides. But God's protection is not only sufficient—it is superior. Believers are instructed to *"take up the shield of faith, with which you can extinguish all the flaming arrows of the evil one"* (**Ephesians 6:16**), and to wield *"the sword of the Spirit, which is the word of God"* (**Ephesians 6:17**). The enemy wants us to forfeit that divine protection by stepping out from under it, forgetting that God promises refuge to those who *"dwell in the shelter of the Most High"* (**Psalm 91:1**).

DISCOURAGEMENT AND DESPAIR

Satan works to undermine our hope by bringing circumstances that lead to discouragement and despair. When facing prolonged trials, unanswered prayers, or ongoing challenges, believers may begin to question God's goodness, timing, or even His presence. His strategy aims to gradually erode faith and cause believers to give up on God. Satan knows that "*hope deferred makes the heart sick*" (**Proverbs 13:12**) and uses this principle to weaken spiritual resolve and perseverance. Scripture encourages believers to "*not grow weary in doing good, for in due season we will reap, if we do not give up*" (**Galatians 6:9**). By maintaining an eternal perspective, remembering God's faithfulness in the past, surrounding oneself with encouraging believers, and focusing on God's promises rather than present circumstances, we can "*hold fast the confession of our hope without wavering, for He who promised is faithful*" (**Hebrews 10:23**). Meditate on Scriptures that affirm God's character as a powerful antidote to discouragement.

BUSYNESS AND SPIRITUAL NEGLECT

A subtle but effective strategy is overwhelming believers with busyness and activity, even with good things—to the point that they neglect their spiritual disciplines and relationship with God. This tactic doesn't rely on tempting believers with obvious sin but distracts them with the demands and pace of life until prayer, Bible study, worship, and fellowship are gradually crowded out. Jesus warned about this in the parable of the sower, speaking of the seed that fell among thorns: "*the cares of this world and the deceitfulness of riches choke the word, and it proves unfruitful*" (**Matthew 13:22**). The solution is found in Jesus' example of prioritizing time with the Father and His teaching that "*only one thing is needed*" (**Luke 10:42**). Believers must intentionally protect time for spiritual nourishment, practice regular Sabbath rest, and evaluate their commitments.

COMPLACENCY AND LUKEWARMNESS

Satan often subtly leads believers into spiritual complacency, where they become satisfied with a nominal faith that lacks fervor or commitment. This lukewarm state was strongly addressed in Christ's letter to the Laodicean church: "*I know your deeds, that you are neither cold nor hot. I wish you were either one or the other! So, because you are lukewarm—neither hot nor cold—I am about to spit you out of my mouth*" (**Revelation 3:15–16**). This dangerous spiritual condition causes believers to drift away from their first love for Christ and become ineffective in their witness and service. When we grow comfortable in our faith without hungering for a deeper relationship with God, we become vulnerable to the enemy's influence. As Jesus warned, "*Because of the increase of wickedness, the love of most will grow cold*" (**Matthew 24:12**). Believers must heed Paul's exhortation to "*examine yourselves to see whether you are in the faith; test yourselves*" (**2 Corinthians 13:5**), regularly assessing their spiritual temperature to avoid the deadly trap of complacency.

UNFORGIVENESS AND BITTERNESS

Satan works to trap believers in unforgiveness and bitterness, knowing these emotional states create strongholds that hinder spiritual growth and damage relationships. Paul warns believers to forgive "*in order that Satan might not outwit us. For we are not unaware of his schemes*" (**2 Corinthians 2:10–11**). Harboring bitterness gives the enemy a foothold. Scripture cautions, "S*ee to it that no one falls short of the grace of God and that no bitter root grows up to cause trouble and defile many*" (**Hebrews 12:15**). When we refuse to forgive others, we block our own connection to God's forgiveness and give Satan a right to directly influence our lives. Jesus emphasized the importance of forgiveness for a believer, teaching that we must "*forgive others to receive forgiveness ourselves*" (**Matthew 6:14–15**). The enemy knows that unforgiveness creates a prison that holds both the offended and the offender captive, which is why Jesus taught us to pray, "*forgive us our debts, as we also have forgiven our debtors*" (**Matthew 6:12**), making our own forgiveness contingent on our willingness to forgive others.

SELF-RIGHTEOUSNESS

Satan encourages believers to develop a sense of self-righteousness, leading them to trust in their own religious performance rather than in Christ's righteousness. This deceptive strategy creates a form of godliness that lacks genuine spiritual power. As Paul warned, "*having a form of godliness but denying its power*" (**2 Timothy 3:5**). Self-righteousness leads to pride, judgment of others, and blindness to one's own sin and need for God's grace, mercy, and forgiveness. Jesus strongly condemned this attitude in the Pharisees, warning, "*Woe to you, teachers of the law and Pharisees, you hypocrites! You are like whitewashed tombs, which look beautiful on the outside but on the inside are full of the bones of the dead and everything unclean*" (**Matthew 23:27**). This spiritual blindness prevents genuine repentance and blocks the transformation of the Holy Spirit into Christ's image. A self-righteous person falls into the trap Jesus described in the parable of the Pharisee and the tax collector, where the Pharisee "*trusted in himself that he was righteous and looked down on everyone else*" (Luke 18:9), revealing how this attitude severs our connection to God's grace.

NARCISSISTIC MANIPULATION

Satan often employs individuals with narcissistic traits as potent vessels to execute his schemes against believers. These "*wolves in sheep's clothing*" (**Matthew 7:15**) possess a dangerous combination of charm, manipulation, and an insatiable hunger for admiration that makes them particularly effective instruments in spiritual warfare. The Bible describes them as "*lovers of self*" (**2 Timothy 3:2**), having "*haughty eyes and a proud heart*" (**Proverbs 21:4**), and being "*wise in their own eyes*" (**Proverbs 26:12**).
(See the next page for a deeper look into this particular strategy)

SATAN'S MANIPULATION THROUGH HUMAN VESSELS

Satan strategically uses narcissistic individuals—especially against believers who exhibit the fruits of the Spirit like empathy, compassion, and kindness. These individuals become destructive instruments in spiritual warfare, causing deep harm while maintaining a façade of righteousness. Scripture warns of such people as "*having the appearance of godliness, but denying its power*" (**2 Timothy 3:5**), and those who "b*y smooth talk and flattery deceive the hearts of the naive*" (**Romans 16:18**).

Christian counselors confirm that narcissists often target emotionally sensitive people, exploiting their compassion as weakness. Dr. Chuck DeGroat, theologian and counselor, observes that narcissistic abuse causes not only emotional damage but a spiritual wound; distorting one's ability to trust God. This form of psychological abuse attacks the very foundation of a believer's faith.

The tactics used by narcissists closely mirror Satan's strategies:

Gaslighting and Deception - Just as satan is the "*father of lies*" **John 8:44**, they distort reality, causing victims to question their perceptions, memories, and even sanity. This creates profound confusion that parallels satan's strategy of deception.

False Righteousness - Like Satan who "*disguises himself as an angel of light*" **2 Corinthians 11:14**, they maintain a carefully crafted public image of virtue while operating in darkness privately. Jesus condemned this hypocrisy as "*whitewashed tombs*" **Matthew 23:27**.

Division and Isolation - Satan seeks to "*divide and devour*" **1 Peter 5:8.** They systematically isolate their targets from supportive relationships, creating triangulation and turning people against one another, directly fulfilling satan's goal of destroying unity.

Accusation and Shame - As "*accuser of the brethren*" **Revelation 12:10**, satan works through them to heap condemnation, criticism, and shame, especially on believers actively pursuing their God-given purpose.

Pride and Self-exaltation - Reflecting satan's original sin of pride, they exhibit an inflated sense of importance and entitlement that contradicts Christ's call to humility. "*God opposes the proud but gives grace to the humble*" **James 4:6**.

Scripture Twisting - Just as satan misquoted Scripture when tempting Jesus **Matthew 4:6**, they weaponize Bible verses to control, silence and manipulate, ignoring teachings on repentance, accountability and fruits of the Spirit.

This spiritual abuse damages the victim's relationship with God, leading them to question His goodness and protection—precisely the doubts Satan aims to sow. Subjecting a person to ongoing deception, control, and emotional abuse while claiming to represent godliness creates profound spiritual confusion. These "*wolves in sheep's clothing*" thrive in communities where grace is emphasized but discernment is underdeveloped. Jesus said, "*You will recognize them by their fruits*" (**Matthew 7:16**). The stark contrast between their words and actions provides the discernment Jesus offers. Look at consistent patterns of behavior (fruit), rather than persuasive words or occasional gestures.

148

STRONGHOLDS

Christians can have strongholds they aren't even aware of. Strongholds are deeply entrenched patterns of negative thinking and behavior based on lies we've accepted that oppose God's truth, distort our perception, and hinder spiritual growth. Often rooted in childhood, strongholds shape our actions and obstruct our purpose and obedience to God. These deceptions, false beliefs, and sin patterns can keep us in bondage and prevent us from walking in the full freedom Jesus came to give.

A common example is the belief formed from childhood abuse: *"I must protect myself because God did not protect me."* This mindset becomes a stronghold when abuse triggers long-term hypervigilance and self-preservation, driven by fight, flight, or freeze survival responses. While these reactions may have once protected us, they can harden into patterns that prevent full trust in God. The path to freedom involves learning to rely on God's protection instead of our own. Trusting His promises and embracing His care enables us to break free from these patterns and experience greater peace.

God invites us to come to Him so He can tear down every stronghold. Go to Him in prayer, asking for help to identify areas of recurring sin, negative patterns, or lies that contradict His truth. These may involve internal struggles or external pressures. As we acknowledge these strongholds, God gives us the strength to overcome through prayer, Scripture, and the support of others.

1. Identify a current stronghold or temptation you are facing.

2. Reflect on it's root—fear, insecurity, doubt or something else.

3. Write down a scripture that speaks to this struggle.

4. Create a prayer addressing the issue and ask God for strength, including one practical step to move toward freedom.

_____

_____

_____

_____

"Your purpose is found at the intersection of *God's glory and your joy.*"

John Piper

CHAPTER 14

Our Divine Authority in Christ

OUR DIVINE AUTHORITY

When embracing our God-given purpose, we must understand the authority we have in Christ. Without this understanding, we may struggle to walk in the freedom Jesus won for us and to stand strong against the darkness that still tries to overshadow that victory. Satan and his demonic forces are real enemies, actively seeking to thwart God's plans and purposes for our lives. They operate in the spiritual realm, where traditional weapons and natural defenses are ineffective. This is why knowing our spiritual authority in Christ—along with the weapons God has given us AND how to use them—is essential for standing firm in our faith and living without fear. **Ephesians 6:10 - 12** *"Finally, be strong in the Lord and in the strength of his might. Put on the whole armor of God, that you may be able to stand against the schemes of the devil. For we do not wrestle against flesh and blood, but against the rulers, against the authorities, against the cosmic powers over this present darkness, against the spiritual forces of evil in the heavenly places."* The phrase *"heavenly places"* refers to a spiritual dimension where both God's Kingdom and the forces of darkness operate. As believers, we are spiritually *"seated with Christ in the heavenly places"* (**Ephesians 2:6**), where Jesus is enthroned. Our exalted position in Him means we are united with Him, sharing in His triumph over Satan, sin, and death. We have been given authority over all the power of the enemy who seeks to invade our lives. From this place of authority in Christ, we are not fighting for victory—we are standing in it. We engage in spiritual warfare not from a place of defeat, but from the position of Christ's finished work. While the ultimate victory belongs to the Lord, He calls us to stand firm and enforce that victory in our daily lives. Scripture equips us to resist fear and empowers us to fight from victory, not for it. Being seated with Him symbolizes not just our spiritual position, but also the authority and inheritance we possess as children of God. Trusting in God's sovereignty and the authority He has given us allows us to face every spiritual storm and emerge victorious. In Christ, we are more than conquerors, empowered to overcome darkness day by day. The authority we have been given comes from Jesus Christ, the King of kings and Lord of Lords. Before His ascension, Jesus declared, *"All authority in heaven and on earth has been given to Me"* **Matthew 28:18**. He then conferred this authority to His followers. *"I have given you authority to trample on snakes and scorpions and to overcome all the power of the enemy; nothing will harm you."* **Luke 10:19** As believers, we have the authority to stand against and defeat the works of the enemy. This authority does not mean we should take unnecessary risks. We must still exercise wisdom and discernment in our actions and know how to use the name of Jesus effectively. If believers are unaware of their spiritual authority, they are more vulnerable to satan's attacks. This can lead to a defeated mindset, where believers feel powerless against the enemy. We are no match against satan, or demonic influences, but it's crucial to understand the spiritual battle that we face as Christian women is real. We have been given practical instructions and can effectively wield the weapons we've been given through God's power and the authority we have in Jesus Christ over the enemy. **1 John 4:4** tells us, *"Greater is He that is within us than he that is in the world."* Understanding the nature of the spiritual forces of wickedness in high places, we can engage effectively only when we know what is expected of us. *"For though we live in the world, we do not wage war as the world does. The weapons of our warfare are not worldly but have divine power to destroy strongholds. We destroy arguments and every lofty opinion raised against the knowledge of God, and take every thought captive to obey Christ."* **2 Corinthians 10:3–5**

The spiritual battle we wage is primarily in our minds. The enemy strategically uses our painful past wounds to plant false narratives and establish footholds of deception, attempting to lead us into agreement with lies that contradict our identity in Christ. Satan is *"a liar and the father of lies"* (**John 8:44**). Yet through our position in Christ, we have been given authority against these deceptions. By standing firm in God's truth, we can expose and dispel every falsehood the enemy has constructed in our minds. Our true battle is not against flesh and blood but against spiritual forces that seek to obstruct God's purpose for our lives.

These dark, evil spiritual entities influence humans created in God's image by exploiting our weaknesses, fears, and insecurities—leading us to act in ways that cause harm to others through our words and actions or them to us. By manipulating people, words and actions provoke conflicts, amplify misunderstandings, and create obstacles to our spiritual growth and fulfillment. While people may choose to hurt us, it is ultimately these spiritual forces that orchestrate such harm to disrupt our path and thwart God's plans. That doesn't release people from responsibility, but it does give us a clear understanding of the strategies of the true enemy of our soul and emphasizes the importance of knowing the authority we possess and the strategies we need to counteract his attacks.

Our position in Christ grants us divine authority over all the enemy's schemes, whether they come directly from spiritual forces or through human vessels. As we grow in understanding this authority, we learn to exercise it with both wisdom and power knowing when to confront, when to withdraw, and how to maintain our spiritual integrity in all circumstances. The Holy Spirit equips us with spiritual discernment to recognize when others might be used as instruments in spiritual warfare, ensuring that *"we are not ignorant of his [Satan's] schemes"* (**2 Corinthians 2:11**). This authority is not merely defensive but empowers us to advance God's Kingdom purposes in our lives and in the lives of others.

Our authority in Christ is absolute, but we must learn to wield it effectively. Like a police officer whose authority comes from their badge and the government behind them, our authority comes from our position in Christ and the power of God working through us. When we speak and act in alignment with God's Word and will, we exercise this authority to overcome every obstacle the enemy places in our path.

Woman of God

You are called to be a warrior who engages in the spiritual realm, not just a mere recipient of God's divine grace. We must remain vigilant, actively standing firm against the enemy's schemes and using the spiritual weapons outlined in **Ephesians Chapter 6**

Every woman has been given spiritual weapons and strategies

CHAPTER 15

The Armor of God

"For we do not wrestle against flesh and blood, but against the rulers, against the authorities, against the cosmic powers over this present darkness, against the spiritual forces of evil in the heavenly places."

~Ephesians 6:12

ARMOR OF GOD

A significant battle occurs in our minds through our thoughts, beliefs, and attitudes. Understanding and applying the spiritual weapons God has provided is crucial for fully engaging in spiritual warfare to overcome our adversary, the devil. We possess weapons far superior to anything the world can offer. Our instruction manual, the Bible, clarifies our position, tells us our marching orders, reveals who we are in Christ, and shows us how to claim the victory that's already been won. We must daily equip ourselves spiritually with the full armor of God. Each piece of this divine protection and weaponry is necessary for standing firm and positioning us for victory against the enemy's assaults, as outlined in **Ephesians 6:11**. Ideally, we should never take off this armor. When we put it on each morning, we affirm the authority and identity we already have, rooted in Christ. By wielding the weapon of faith and trusting in God's promise to protect us, we experience the freedom and fulfillment of our God-given purpose and can use our weapons to advance God's Kingdom. The power behind the armor of God is not our own; it is God's might working through us. By daily securing each piece of our armor, we invite God to take command of our battles in an act of faith, declaring that our victory is secured not by our own efforts, but by the power and authority of the One who has overcome the world. This perspective shifts our focus from self-reliance to divine dependence, grounding us in the reality that God is the true source of our strength and success. Modeled after a Roman soldier's gear, this armor is a powerful symbol of the protection and authority we have in Christ. Each piece is necessary for survival and victory in the battle. By consciously dressing spiritually for the day, we ensure that we are protected from the enemy's schemes, standing firm as our battle is fought in the heavenlies. As warriors in Christ's army, equipped with His battle gear, we are reminded that we are part of something far greater than ourselves, focusing on our mission and the Great Commission as rightful daughters of the King. This armor protects and empowers us to take an active stand against the enemy, advancing God's Kingdom with courage and conviction. We must be sober-minded and vigilant since our adversary prowls around like a lion, seeking whom he may devour. But in all these things, we are more than conquerors through Him who loved us. This truth emboldens us to face each day with confidence, knowing that we have everything we need to stand firm in our faith, facing any challenge to fulfill our purpose with unwavering resolve.

We can actively resist the devil's schemes with vigilance and perseverance. By continually renewing our minds with God's truth and immersing ourselves in His Word, we reinforce our defense against the enemy and fortify our spiritual resilience. When we step out of our own strength and reliance and step into His strength, depending on Him, we shift from our human abilities to His divine power, which is far greater. This perspective humbles us and keeps our focus on God as the true source of our victory.

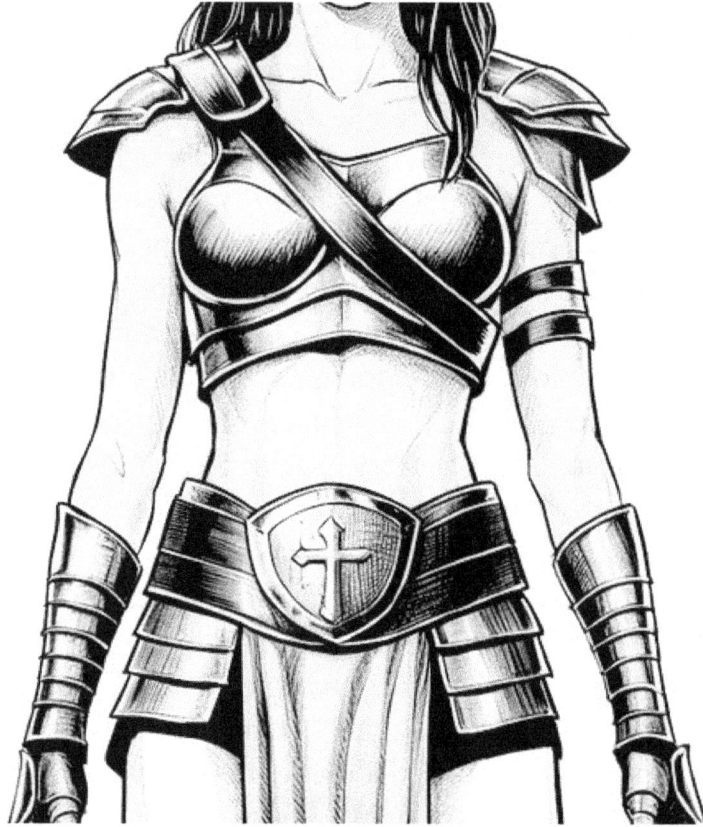

THE BELT OF TRUTH

In Roman warfare, the belt was a crucial piece of the soldier's armor. It secured the soldier's tunic and held the scabbard, the sheath for the sword. The belt provided stability and readiness, ensuring that the soldier was not encumbered and could move freely in battle. Without the belt, the armor would be incomplete, and the soldier would be vulnerable and unprepared. The belt was often adorned with small decorative pieces symbolizing the soldier's rank and achievements, serving as a visible reminder of his identity and role within the army. This belt was not only functional but also a symbol of the soldier's readiness and commitment to the cause he fought for.

Spiritual Application: The Belt of Truth represents the foundational truth of God's Word and the truth of who we are in Christ. Just as the Roman soldier's belt secured all other pieces of armor, the truth of God's Word holds everything together in the spiritual battle. For a Christian woman, this means grounding herself in the truth of Scripture and standing firm against the lies and deceptions of the enemy. By embracing truth, she can live confidently, knowing who she is in Christ and standing strong against the falsehoods and accusations the enemy might hurl her way. The Belt of Truth is not just about knowing the truth intellectually; it's about living it out daily, letting it shape every thought, decision, and action. In doing so, she is protected and empowered to stand strong, unshaken by the enemy's schemes, and fully equipped to fulfill her God-given purpose.

BREASTPLATE
OF RIGHTEOUSNESS

The breastplate was one of the most vital pieces of armor for a Roman soldier, protecting the vital organs, especially the heart from fatal blows. Made of metal, it covered the torso, guarding the soldier from arrows, swords, and other weapons. Without it, a soldier would be left vulnerable to the enemy's attacks, unable to survive in the heat of battle. The breastplate was often custom-fitted to ensure maximum protection and mobility, allowing the soldier to engage in combat without being hindered. This piece of armor symbolized the soldier's readiness to face the enemy, fully shielded from potentially deadly strikes.

Spiritual Application:

The Breastplate of Righteousness represents the righteousness given to us through Jesus Christ. In spiritual warfare, it protects our hearts from the accusations, guilt, and shame that the enemy tries to inflict. For a Christian woman, this breastplate serves as a reminder that she is made righteous through Christ, not by her own efforts. By living in this righteousness and maintaining a pure heart, she guards against the enemy's attempts to wound her with feelings of unworthiness or failure. It allows her to walk confidently into battle, knowing she is clothed in Christ's righteousness. This gives her the assurance to stand firm in her faith, knowing her heart's protected by Christ's righteousness and God's grace, enabling her to resist the enemy's attempts to undermine her identity. 159

THE SHOES OF THE GOSPEL

The Shoes of the Gospel of the readiness of peace are not just shoes; they represent an attitude and characteristics of the spirit of Jesus Christ. Roman soldiers wore sandals known as caligae, which were designed for stability and mobility in battle. These sandals had thick soles and were often fitted with nails or studs to provide a firm grip on the ground. This design allowed the soldier to stand firm in combat and march long distances without fear of slipping or losing footing, making them essential for maintaining their position and advancing against the enemy. The caligae were not just practical but also symbolized the soldier's readiness to face any terrain or challenge, ensuring that he could remain steadfast and unshaken in the heat of battle.

Spiritual Application:

The Shoes of the Gospel of Peace symbolize the readiness and stability that come from the peace of Christ. In spiritual warfare, having peace allows a Christian woman to stand firm and move forward without fear or anxiety. This peace is rooted in the good news of the gospel, reminding her that she is reconciled with God and can walk confidently in her faith. Just as the caligae provided soldiers with the ability to stand firm and advance, the peace of Christ enables her to move forward with unwavering stability. By being grounded in this peace, she can face the trials and challenges of life with a calm and steady heart, knowing that she is firmly anchored in the promises of God. This spiritual footing ensures that she remains steadfast in her journey, regardless of the obstacles or adversities she encounters.

SHIELD OF FAITH

The Romans used a large, curved rectangular shield known as the scutum, which was designed to protect the soldier's entire body. Made from wood and covered with leather, these shields were often soaked in water before battle. This strategic move would extinguish the flaming arrows upon impact, as enemy forces commonly used arrows dipped in pitch and set on fire; called fiery darts. Soldiers would link their shields together in a "testudo" (turtle formation), creating an almost impenetrable barrier with shields covering them from head to toe. This strategic defense was a particularly effective move against a barrage of arrows, protecting the entire unit as they advanced together in unity.

Spiritual Application:

In the spiritual battle, the Shield of Faith is a vital piece of the Armor of God. Just as a Roman soldier's shield protected him from physical attacks, the Shield of Faith protects believers from the spiritual assaults of the enemy, specifically the fiery darts of Satan. These darts can take the form of doubts, fears, temptations, and lies aimed at weakening our faith and trust in God. This shield represents unwavering confidence in God's promises and power. When we soak our faith in the living water of God's Word and trust in His faithfulness, our shield becomes impenetrable to the enemy's attacks. As the Roman shield extinguished physical flames, our faith extinguishes spiritual flaming arrows, enabling us to stand firm in the face of trials, fears, and adversities. By holding up the Shield of Faith, we are equipped to deflect and extinguish every attack that comes our way, remaining steadfast in our journey with Christ. Our faith is strengthened through community and unity in trusting God alongside other believers.

161

HELMET OF SALVATION

The Roman helmet, or galea, was a crucial piece of armor designed to offer comprehensive protection to a soldier's head. Crafted from metal, it featured a sturdy construction that shielded the head from direct blows and projectiles. Helmets often included a faceplate, cheek guards, and sometimes even a neck guard to provide additional defense. This protective gear was essential in close combat scenarios, where injuries to the head could be fatal or debilitating. The design not only provided physical protection but also instilled a sense of confidence in the soldier, knowing that one of the most vulnerable parts of the body was well-guarded.

Spiritual Application: The helmet of salvation (**Ephesians 6:17**) represents the protective assurance of our salvation in Christ, shielding our minds from spiritual attacks. Just as the Roman helmet safeguarded soldiers from physical injuries, this spiritual armor guards us against doubts, fears, and uncertainties about our eternal security. By protecting our minds, (having the mind of Christ) we can think clearly and make decisions based on faith rather than fear. Embracing the certainty of our salvation helps us resist the enemy's attempts to sow confusion and despair. By continually reminding ourselves of our secure position in Christ, we can maintain a stable and confident mindset, fully equipped to face spiritual challenges with assurance and peace. This mental and spiritual protection is crucial for remaining steadfast in our faith, allowing us to navigate life's battles with the knowledge that our ultimate victory is secured in Christ— both salvation and our minds.

SWORD OF THE SPIRIT

The Roman sword, or gladius, was a formidable weapon used in close combat, distinguished by its short, double-edged blade. This design allowed Roman soldiers to engage enemies with precision and effectiveness, making quick thrusts and powerful slashes. The gladius was a critical tool for both offensive strikes and defensive maneuvers, enabling soldiers to navigate the chaos of battle with agility and control. Its effectiveness was a key factor in the military success of the Roman legions. This weapon was not only a tool of combat but also a symbol of authority and discipline, embodying the strength and resolve of the Roman soldier in the face of adversity.

Spiritual Application:

The sword of the Spirit (**Ephesians 6:17**), which is the Word of God, functions as a powerful tool for spiritual warfare. Just as the Roman weapon was essential for close combat, the Word of God is vital for confronting and overcoming spiritual challenges. It allows believers to counter the enemy's deceptions, temptations, and lies with divine truth. The scriptures equip us to respond effectively to spiritual attacks, offering both defense and offense in the battle against darkness. Regularly studying and meditating on the Bible strengthens our ability to wield this spiritual weapon with skill and confidence. We are not passive participants but are called to actively engage in proclaiming the truth of God's Word aloud, as Jesus did, while standing firm against Satan's schemes, strategies, and strikes.

PRAYER

In Roman military operations, effective communication was crucial for coordinating movements and strategies. Soldiers relied on a variety of signals, from visual cues to verbal commands, to ensure that their actions were synchronized and responsive to the enemy's tactics. This communication network enabled troops to execute complex maneuvers and adapt to changing battle conditions. Without such coordination, the effectiveness of the Roman army would have been significantly diminished. The ability to convey information quickly and accurately often determined the outcome of battles, showcasing the importance of unity and clarity in achieving victory.

Spiritual Application: Prayer serves as our primary means of communication with God, akin to the Roman army's communication system. It enables believers to seek divine guidance, strength, and support in the midst of spiritual battles. As **Ephesians 6:18** emphasizes, prayer should be persistent and encompass all aspects of our lives. Through prayer, we maintain a vital connection with God, receiving His direction and encouragement. It allows us to express our needs, seek His intervention, and align our will with His purposes, ensuring that we remain spiritually attuned and fortified against the enemy's schemes. In this way, consistent prayer not only strengthens our faith but also empowers us to face challenges with confidence, knowing that we are supported by God and His wisdom and power.

CHAPTER 16

Our Spiritual Strategies

SPIRITUAL STRATEGIES

We are told to *"submit to God, resist the devil, and he will flee from us"* (**James 4:7**).

When we submit to God, we voluntarily place ourselves under His protection. Only then can we resist the devil. How do we do that? By taking our thoughts captive, praying, using Scripture, and exercising the authority given to us. We can verbally tell him to *"get behind us in Jesus' name."* With every temptation, God provides everything we need when we go to Him. *"No temptation has overtaken you that is not common to man. God is faithful, and He will not let you be tempted beyond your ability, but with the temptation, He will also provide the way of escape, that you may be able to endure it"* (**1 Corinthians 10:13**).

We have been given the power to dismantle strongholds by *"taking every thought captive to the obedience of Christ"* (**2 Corinthians 10:5**) and all authority in the name of Jesus.

We follow these commands through spiritual disciplines such as prayer to maintain a strong connection with God, memorizing Scripture, being mindful of our thoughts, replacing negativity with God's truth, expressing gratitude, focusing on Christ, and seeking accountability. Only then can we resist the enemy's attacks effectively. God, in His omniscience, understood that human nature inclines toward negative thoughts that can add to the warfare we encounter in our minds. Scripture provides specific guidance on cultivating a positive and righteous mindset. The Bible serves as a comprehensive guidebook, instructing us on how to overcome this natural tendency. **Philippians 4:8** directs us: *"Whatever is true, whatever is honorable, whatever is just, whatever is pure, whatever is lovely, whatever is commendable, if there is any excellence, if there is anything worthy of praise, think about these things."*

We are *"not to be conformed to this world but to be transformed by the renewing of our minds"* (**Romans 12:2**). Renewing our minds is done by memorizing and reading God's Word.

Because Jesus overcame Satan, we too are overcomers. Because Jesus already won the victory, we are victorious. Because He won, we are winners and warriors as we stand firm on the truth of the Gospel. Because He conquered, we are more than conquerors. His triumph is our ultimate assurance. His victory is our foundation for confidence. Our role in continuing what He won for us is to appropriate His victory through faith and obedience, through the Holy Spirit who resides and dwells within us, empowering us to overcome the world's temptations and the enemy's schemes. To do that, we need to know the tools we have been given and the strategies to counteract Satan's schemes. Like anyone who fights in battle, they need to be armed with the weapons of warfare (armor of God) and have basic training to stand against the enemy. On the following pages, you will learn the strategies you need, to know how to walk in victory against the enemy of your soul.

STAND FIRM IN GOD'S WORD

The Bible is your ultimate weapon. Meditate on it and let God's Word transform and renew your mind. Memorize scriptures that speak to your specific needs and challenges and speak God's Word aloud over each circumstance. Use your authority in Christ.

DECLARE GOD'S PROMISES

Declare God's promise aloud over your life. Jesus used scripture to counter Satan's temptations in the wilderness. **Matthew 4:1-11** and rebuked Peter when he spoke under satan's influence **Matthew 16:23**

Example: *"I declare that the peace of God guards my heart and mind in Christ Jesus"* Philippians 4:7.

AUTHORITY AGAINST SATAN

We have authority in Christ to *"resist the devil, and he will flee"* **James 4:7**. Jesus demonstrated this for us. This is a powerful defense against spiritual deception and attack and to get satan to leave.

Example: *"Get behind me, Satan!" in Jesus' name.*

CANCEL THE ENEMY'S ASSIGNMENTS

Use the authority you've been given to break the power of the enemy's plans.

Example: *"I cancel every assignment of the enemy in my life, family, friends and finances, in Jesus' name."*

DECLARE AND USE THE NAME OF JESUS

Using the name of Jesus carries immense power at the end of your prayers. Use His name.

Example: *"I come against this situation in the name of Jesus. You have no power here!"*

ASK FOR PROTECTION

God desires to protect His children. Ask for His covering over yourself, your family, and your circumstances.

Example: *"Father, I ask for Your hedge of protection around me and my loved ones."*

PLEAD THE BLOOD OF JESUS

The blood of Jesus defeated Satan and brings protection and deliverance.

Example: *"I plead the blood of Jesus over my mind, body, and spirit. No weapon formed against me shall prosper"* **Isaiah 54:17**.

ACTIVATE YOUR FAITH

Believe in the promises of God. Faith is the currency of the spiritual realm.

Example: *"I choose to believe God for healing, provision, and breakthrough."*

REBUKE FEAR

Fear is a tool of the enemy. "God has not given us a spirit of fear, but of power, love, and a sound mind" 2 Timothy 1:7.

Example: *"I rebuke fear in Jesus' name. I will not be shaken because God is with me."*

PROCLAIM GOD'S SOVEREIGNTY

Affirm God's control over your life and circumstances, declaring that His will shall prevail.

Example: *"Lord, You are sovereign over all. I trust You with every aspect of my life. Let Your will be done."*

ARMOR UP

Put on the full armor of God daily **Ephesians 6:10-18** to stand firm against the enemy's schemes. As you dress in the morning imagine yourself securing each piece.

Example: *"I have on the helmet of salvation, the breastplate of righteousness, the belt of truth, and the shoes of the gospel of peace. I take up the shield of faith and the sword of the Spirit, which is the Word of God."*

SPIRITUAL DISCERNMENT

Ask God for wisdom to discern the enemy's schemes and distinguish between truth and deception. This is a critical defensive measure against spiritual attacks. *"But solid food is for the mature, who by constant use have trained themselves to distinguish good from evil"* **Hebrews 5:14**.

Example: *"Holy Spirit, give me discernment to recognize the enemy's tactics and deception in this situation."*

WORSHIP AS WARFARE

Worship shifts the spiritual atmosphere and invites God's presence, which the enemy cannot withstand. When Paul and Silas worshiped in prison, God moved powerfully on their behalf. The prison doors opened. **Acts 16:25-26**.

Example: *"I choose to worship You, Lord, in the midst of this battle, knowing Your presence dispels darkness."*

STRATEGIC FASTING

Jesus taught that some spiritual battles require fasting in addition to prayer. This spiritual discipline intensifies our connection with God and breaks strongholds. *"This kind can come out only by prayer and fasting"* **Mark 9:29**

Example: *"Lord, I dedicate this fast to You, asking for breakthrough in this spiritual struggle."*

CORPORATE PRAYER

Join with other believers in prayer, as there is multiplied power in united faith. Jesus promised His presence when believers gather in His name **Matthew 18:19-20**.

Example: *"Father, we come together in agreement, binding the spirit of division in our family in Jesus' name."*

THANKSGIVING AND PRAISE

Gratitude is a powerful weapon that shifts your focus from the problem to the Problem-Solver. "*In everything give thanks; for this is God's will for you in Christ Jesus*" (**1 Thessalonians 5:18).**

Example: "*I thank You, Lord, for Your faithfulness even in this trial. I praise You because You are greater than what I face.*"

PRAYER IN THE SPIRIT

Praying in tongues builds up your faith and allows the Holy Spirit to intercede through you according to God's perfect will. "*Pray in the Spirit on all occasions with all kinds of prayers and requests*" (**Ephesians 6:18)**.

Example: Take time to pray in the Spirit, especially when you don't know how to pray about a situation.

BREAK SOUL TIES

Sever unhealthy spiritual connections that may give the enemy access to your life. "*Do not be yoked together with unbelievers*" (**2 Corinthians 6:14)**.

Example: "*In Jesus' name, I break every unhealthy soul tie formed through [specific relationship/situation], and I declare myself free.*"

BINDING AND LOOSING

Exercise the spiritual authority Jesus gave believers to bind evil influences and loose God's purposes. "*Whatever you bind on earth will be bound in heaven, and whatever you loose on earth will be loosed in heaven*" (**Matthew 18:18)**.

Example: "*I bind the spirit of anxiety affecting my mind, and I loose peace, clarity, and sound judgment in Jesus' name.*"

RESPONDING TO NARCISSISTIC MANIPULATION

Jesus demonstrated perfect wisdom in responding to those who sought to manipulate, control, and harm Him and His mission. When confronted by those who twisted truth and harbored harmful intentions, Jesus sometimes remained silent **(Matthew 27:12-14)**, spoke direct truth **(Matthew 23)**, or simply removed Himself from their presence **(John 8:59)**. Each response was strategic rather than reactive. Jesus's command to be "*wise as serpents and innocent as doves*" **(Matthew 10:16)** provides our framework for responding to narcissistic manipulation as a form of spiritual warfare.

(**See the next page for a deeper look into this particular strategy)**

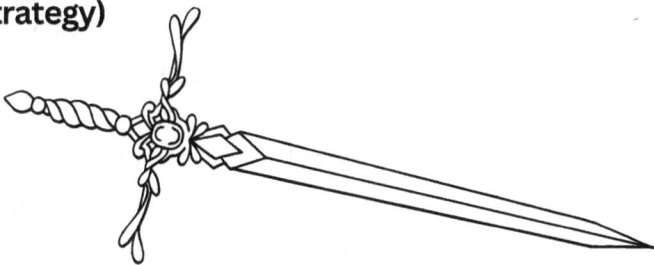

SPECIFIC STRATEGIES FOR NARCISSISTIC ENCOUNTERS
EXERCISE SPIRITUAL DISCERNMENT

Jesus taught us to recognize people by their "fruit" **(Matthew 7:16-20)** rather than their words or religious appearance. The Holy Spirit grants believers discernment to recognize deception and manipulation. "*Beloved, do not believe every spirit, but test the spirits to see whether they are from God*" **(1 John 4:1).**

Example Prayer: "Holy Spirit, sharpen my discernment to recognize the tactics of manipulation and deception. Help me see clearly without becoming suspicious of everyone."

Example Action: Keep a journal documenting patterns of behavior, noting inconsistencies between words and actions, broken promises, and manipulation tactics. Look for the fruits of the Spirit **(Galatians 5:22-23)** or their absence.

IMPLEMENT BOUNDARIES WITH BIBLICAL WISDOM

Jesus established clear boundaries in His interactions. He knew when to engage and when to withdraw, when to speak and when to remain silent. Paul instructed believers to "*have nothing to do with such people*" **(2 Timothy 3:5)** regarding those who had an appearance of godliness but denied its power.

Example Declaration: "I establish this boundary not out of unforgiveness, but as an act of stewardship over the peace, purpose, and calling God has given me."

Example Strategy: Define specific, measurable boundaries (e.g., "I will not engage in conversations about sensitive topics with this person" or "I will only interact in group settings, not one-on-one").

STAND FIRM IN YOUR IDENTITY IN CHRIST

People with narcissistic behaviors attempt to define your identity and worth based on their shifting perceptions and need for control. Counter this by anchoring yourself firmly in what God says about you. "*But you are a chosen race, a royal priesthood, a holy nation, a people for his own possession*" **(1 Peter 2:9)**.

Example Practice: Create Scripture cards with verses affirming your identity in Christ. Read them daily, especially before interactions with the person.

Example Declaration: "I am who God says I am—beloved, chosen, forgiven, and called. No human opinion can change my true identity."

PRACTICE LIMITED CONTACT OR NO CONTACT

Paul advised believers to "*as far as it depends on you, live peaceably with all*" **(Romans 12:18)**. Peace isn't always possible. In some cases, creating appropriate distance is biblically sound. Jesus withdrew from those who sought to harm Him **(Luke 4:30)**.

Example Strategy: Communicate boundaries clearly. If violated, reduce contact to minimal interaction or complete separation when necessary. Use the "**gray rock**" method (being as uninteresting and non-reactive as possible) when interaction is unavoidable.

Example Prayer: *"Lord, give me wisdom to know when to engage and when to withdraw, just as Jesus did. Help me create necessary distance without harboring bitterness."*

COUNTER GASLIGHTING WITH GOD'S TRUTH

When faced with reality distortion, anchor yourself in God's unchanging truth. *"Sanctify them in the truth; your word is truth"* **(John 17:17)**. God's Word provides a stable reality foundation when others try to manipulate your perceptions.

Example Declaration and Practice: Keep a truth journal documenting events, conversations, and promises to protect yourself from gaslighting and reality distortion. *"God's truth is my foundation. I will not be moved from what I know to be true, regardless of manipulation or contradiction."*

BREAK UNHEALTHY SOUL TIES

Relationships with manipulative people often create unhealthy and ungodly spiritual connections that give the enemy continued access to your thoughts and emotions. These can be broken through prayer and declaration. *"Do not be unequally yoked with unbelievers"* **(2 Corinthians 6:14)** applies to any relationship that pulls you away from God.

Example Prayer: *"Lord Jesus, I break every unhealthy soul tie created through this relationship. I cut off every connection that has given the enemy access to my mind, emotions, and spirit. I rebuke Satan and renounce any ungodly soul tie with _____ and declare myself free in Jesus' name."*

SEEK GODLY COUNSEL AND SUPPORT

Ecclesiastes (4:12) reminds us that *"though one may be overpowered, two can defend themselves"*. Find support from spiritually mature believers who understand manipulative dynamics. *"Where there is no guidance, a people falls, but in an abundance of counselors there is safety"* **(Proverbs 11:14)**.

Example Action: Connect with a Christian counselor specializing in this type of abuse, or join a support group led by those with biblical understanding of these dynamics.

PRACTICE FORGIVENESS WITHOUT COMPROMISING BOUNDARIES

Forgiveness is commanded **(Ephesians 4:32)**, but reconciliation and peace aren't always possible. This requires genuine repentance from both parties. You can release someone to God without restoring the relationship. *"If possible, so far as it depends on you, live peaceably with all"* **(Romans 12:18)**.

Example Prayer: *"Lord, I choose to forgive as an act of obedience and for my own and their freedom. I release my right to revenge and place justice in Your hands, while maintaining the boundaries that protect the calling You've given me."*

RESPOND RATHER THAN REACT

Jesus often responded to manipulation with questions or silence **(Matthew 21:23-27)**. This strategy prevents being drawn into emotional reactions that feed their need for drama and fuel their manipulation, giving you time to align your response with God's love and wisdom.

Example Response: When baited into an argument, practice saying, *"I'll need to think about that and get back to you,"* then disengage to process with God before responding.

FOCUS ON YOUR HEALING AND PURPOSE

Rather than being consumed with the narcissist's behavior, redirect your energy toward fulfilling your God-given purpose. *"Let us run with endurance the race that is set before us, looking to Jesus"* **(Hebrews 12:1-2)**.

Example Commitment: "*I will dedicate daily time to healing practices like Scripture meditation, prayer, counseling, and community support that affirm my worth in Christ and help me reclaim my purpose.*"

USE YOUR SPIRITUAL AUTHORITY

Jesus gave believers authority over "*all the power of the enemy*" **Luke 10:19**. Exercise this authority through declaration, prayer, and standing firm in truth.

Example Declaration: "*In the name of Jesus, I break the power of every lie, manipulation, and evil influence that has operated in this relationship. I declare freedom from these bondages and claim the peace and clarity that Christ has purchased for me.*"

GUARD AGAINST A BITTER ROOT

While establishing boundaries is necessary, be vigilant against allowing bitterness to take root. "*See to it that no one fails to obtain the grace of God; that no "root of bitterness" springs up and causes trouble*" **Hebrews 12:15**.

Example Prayer: "*Search my heart, O God, and reveal any seeds of bitterness, hatred, or unforgiveness. I choose to release this person to Your perfect justice while maintaining the boundaries You've led me to establish.*"

In implementing these strategies, remember that your ultimate battle is not against the person, but against the spiritual forces using them. Your authority in Christ empowers you not only to withstand these attacks but to grow stronger through them, emerging with greater wisdom, compassion, and spiritual maturity.

QUESTIONS FOR REFLECTION:

What signs of manipulative behaviors have I encountered in my relationships, and how might these be part of a larger spiritual battle?

How can I practice Jesus' example of responding to manipulation with wisdom rather than emotional reactions?

What boundaries do I need to establish to protect my spiritual well-being while still showing Christ's love?

In what ways has my understanding of Christian forgiveness been used against me, and how can I develop a more biblically balanced approach?

How can I support other believers who are experiencing narcissistic abuse in their families, workplaces, or church communities?

SPECIFIC STRATEGIES FOR GENDER CONFUSION

Satan strategically targets our gender identity because it strikes at the core of how God created us. Recognize these as spiritual attacks and employ biblical countermeasures to find freedom and clarity for yourself or those you minister to.

IDENTIFY AND REJECT THE ENEMY'S LIES

The enemy plants specific deceptions about gender identity. Counter each lie or deception with God's truth:

Lie: "*Your body doesn't match who you truly are.*"

Truth Declaration: "*I declare that I am fearfully and wonderfully made. My body is not a mistake but a sacred temple designed by God with purpose.*" **Psalm 139:13-14**

Lie: "*You were born in the wrong body.*"

Truth Declaration: "*I was knit together in my mother's womb according to God's perfect design. I reject the lie that God made a mistake with my body. or identity*" **Psalm 139:13-16**

Lie: "*Changing your gender will solve your pain and confusion.*"

Truth Declaration: "*True transformation comes through the renewal of my mind in Christ, not through changing my body or my gender. In Jesus, I become a new creation with a sound mind.*" **Romans 12:2, 2 Corinthians 5:17**

Lie: "*Your feelings determine your gender identity.*"

Truth Declaration: "*I won't be led by deceptive feelings but by God's unchanging truth. The heart is deceitful above all things. God's Word is reliable.*" **Jeremiah 17:9, John 17:17**

BREAK SPIRITUAL STRONGHOLDS OF CONFUSION

Gender confusion involves strongholds that must be torn down with spiritual authority.

Binding Prayer: "*In the name of Jesus Christ, I bind the spirit of gender confusion that has influenced my life. I break its power and declare it has no authority over my identity.*"

Renunciation Prayer: "*I renounce every lie I have believed about my gender identity. I reject any claim the enemy has made on how I see myself. I cancel the enemy's assignment against my God-given design as male/female.*"

Breaking Soul Ties: "*Lord Jesus, I break every unhealthy soul tie created through relationships, social media, the internet or experiences that distorted my view of gender. I cut off every connection that has given the enemy access to how I perceive my identity.*"

TAKE THOUGHTS CAPTIVE

Gender dysphoria often manifests through persistent thoughts that need to be captured and redirected.

Thought Journal Practice: Write down recurring thoughts about gender identity. Next to each one, write a corresponding truth from Scripture.

_____

_____

_____

Example Declaration: "*I demolish arguments and every pretension that sets itself up against the knowledge of God, and I take captive every thought about being the wrong gender and make it obedient to Christ. These thoughts are not from God, and I replace them with the truth of who God created me to be.*" **2 Corinthians 10:5**

CONFESSION AND DECLARATION

Memorize and speak God's truth aloud to break the power of confusion.

"So God created man in His own image, in the image of God He created him; male and female He created them." **Genesis 1:27**

"I praise You, for I am fearfully and wonderfully made. Wonderful are your works; my soul knows it very well." **Psalm 139:14**

"Or do you not know that your body is a temple of the Holy Spirit within you, whom you have from God? You are not your own, for you were bought with a price. So glorify God in your body." **1 Corinthians 6:19–20**

Daily Declaration: *"I am created as male/female in God's image. My biological sex is not a mistake but a divine design. God created me purposefully and intentionally."*

Authority Declaration: *"In Jesus' name, I command every spirit of confusion, deception, and gender distortion to leave me now. I stand firm in my identity as God created me."*

Body Affirmation: *"I accept my body as God's good gift. I receive this gift God has given me. I honor my body as God's temple and reject any urge to alter what He has designed."*

ESTABLISH PROTECTIVE BOUNDARIES

Create spiritual and practical boundaries against influences that reinforce gender confusion.

Media Fast: *"I commit to a 40-day fast from all media and social influences that promote gender fluidity or transition narratives."*

Example Prayer: *"Lord, give me discernment to recognize content and relationships that pull me away from Your design for my gender. Help me establish godly boundaries that protect the identity You've given me."*

Environment Strategy: *"I will surround myself with believers who affirm God's design while expressing compassion for my struggles."*

SEEK HEALING FOR ROOT CAUSES

Address the wounds that may have created vulnerability to gender confusion.

Inner Healing Prayer: *"Jesus, I invite You into the painful memories where my gender identity was wounded. Reveal where trauma has distorted my self-perception, and bring Your healing truth."*

Warfare Declaration: *"I break agreement with the enemy's interpretation of my painful experiences. I cancel how these wounds have been used to distort my gender identity."*

Example Action: Schedule sessions with a Christian counselor who specializes in trauma and identity issues, while continuing to pray against spiritual attacks during the healing.

PUT ON THE NEW SELF

Actively embrace your God-given gender as part of putting on the new self in Christ.

Embracing Prayer: *"Lord, help me embrace the fullness of how You created me as male/female. Show me how to express my gender in healthy, God-honoring ways that reflect Your design."*

Identity Affirmation: *"I clothe myself with my true identity in Christ. I put off confusion and put on clarity. I reject the old patterns of thinking and embrace the truth of who God says I am."*

Practice: Make a list of biblical examples of godly men/women and study how they expressed their God-given gender in ways that honored Him.

STAND UNITED WITH THE BODY OF CHRIST

Isolation increases vulnerability to enemy attacks. Counteract this through spiritual community:

Corporate Prayer: "Father, we come together as believers to stand against the enemy's attack on gender identity. We bind these spirits of confusion in Jesus' name and loose clarity, truth, and freedom."

Support: Connect with a small group of mature believers who can pray with authority when confusion intensifies.

Accountability Declaration: "*I invite trusted believers to speak truth when I begin to believe lies about my identity. I open myself to their loving correction and guidance.*"

Additional Questions for Reflection:
What specific lies about gender has the enemy planted in your thinking?

Which spiritual warfare strategies resonate most with your situation?

How might regular application of these strategies, combined with counseling for root issues, bring greater freedom?

What biblical truths about your identity can become your strongest weapons in this battle?

How can you balance compassion for yourself while firmly standing against the enemy's deceptions?

Remember: This battle is ultimately not against flesh and blood, but against spiritual forces of darkness that seek to distort God's beautiful design. Your victory is assured in Christ, who has already defeated the enemy and offers complete restoration of your true identity.

"When God gives you a vision, He will also *give you what you need to accomplish that vision.*"

Charles Stanley

CHAPTER 17

Discovering Your Spiritual Gifts

IDENTIFYING YOUR SPIRITUAL GIFTS

Spiritual gifts are divine abilities bestowed by the Holy Spirit upon believers in Christ, meant to edify the church and further God's kingdom on earth. In 1 Corinthians 12, Paul likens the church to a body, with Christ as the head, emphasizing that each member has a unique and vital role.

Just as every part of a physical body is essential for optimal functioning, every spiritual gift is crucial for the health and effectiveness of the church. The Holy Spirit distributes these gifts according to His will, equipping believers for specific roles within the church. By identifying and using our spiritual gifts, we align with God's purpose, contribute to the body of Christ, and experience personal spiritual growth.

Take time to pray and seek God's guidance as you identify your spiritual gifts. Consider how they can be used to serve others and to glorify God as you align with His purpose for your life and spiritual growth. This can help you understand your unique role and contributions to the Kingdom of God.

For Further Study:
For a comprehensive list of Bible verses related to each spiritual gift, refer to **Appendix C: Going Deeper "Biblical References for Spiritual Gifts"** at the back of this book on page 223. This appendix provides the full text of relevant scriptures, allowing for in-depth study and reflection on each of them.

Additionally, you can access a free spiritual gifts test at https://giftstest.com

SPIRITUAL GIFTS

Administration 1 Corinthians 12:28	Organizing church event or managing ministry team
Apostleship Ephesians 4:11	Pioneering new ministries and establishing churches
Craftmanship Exodus 31:3-5	Creating artistic works for ministry purposes
Discernment 1 Corinthians 12:10	Recognizing spiritual truth from error
Evangelism Ephesians 4:11	Sharing the gospel effectively with unbelievers
Exhortation Romans 12:8	Encouraging and counseling others in their faith
Faith 1 Corinthians 12:9	Trusting God for the seemingly impossible
Giving Romans 12:8	Contributing resources generously to ministry needs
Healing 1 Corinthians 12:9, 28	Praying for physical and emotional restoration and laying on of hands
Helps 1 Corinthians 12:28	Assisting others in practical ways
Hospitality 1 Peter 4:9	Creating welcoming environments for ministry

SPIRITUAL GIFTS

Intercession Romans 8:26-27	Praying faithfully for others' needs
Knowledge 1 Corinthians 12:8	Understanding and explaining spiritual truths
Leadership Romans 12:8	Guiding others in ministry objectives
Mercy Romans 12:8	Showing compassion to those in need
Miracles 1 Corinthians 12:10, 28	Demonstrating God's supernatural power
Pastoring/Shepherding Ephesians 4:11	Nurturing spiritual growth in others
Prophecy 1 Corinthians 12:10, 28	Speaking timely messages from God
Service Romans 12:7	Meeting practical needs in ministry
Teaching Ephesians 4:11	Clearly explaining biblical truth
Speak/Interpret Tongues 1 Corinthians 12:10, 28	Speaking and translating in unknown languages
Wisdom 1 Corinthians 12:8	Applying spiritual truth to specific situations

SPIRITUAL GIFTS ASSESSMENT QUESTIONS

Rate each question from 0-3

0 = Never/Not at all

1 = Rarely/A little

2 = Sometimes/Somewhat

3 = Often/Very much

Administration

Do you enjoy creating order out of chaos? ____

Are you skilled at delegating tasks and seeing the big picture? ____

Do you naturally see ways to organize people and tasks effectively? ____

Total for Administration: ____

Apostleship

Do you have a passion for pioneering new ministries? ____

Are you drawn to cross-cultural missions? ____

Do you feel called to start new churches or ministries? ____

Total for Apostleship: ____

Craftsmanship

Do you find joy in creating beautiful or useful things? ____

Are you skilled with your hands? ____

Do you use your artistic abilities to serve the church? ____

Total for Craftsmanship: ____

Discernment

Can you often sense when something is not right spiritually? ____ Do others seek your insight on spiritual matters? ____ Can you easily distinguish between spiritual truth and error? ____

Total for Discernment: ____

Evangelism

Do you feel compelled to share your faith with others? ____ Are you effective in helping people understand the gospel? ____ Do you feel energized when telling others about Jesus? ____

Total for Evangelism: ____

SPIRITUAL GIFTS ASSESSMENT QUESTIONS

Exhortation

Do people often seek you out for advice and encouragement? _____

Do you find it natural to motivate others? _____

Do you easily find words to comfort those in difficult situations? _____

Total for Exhortation: _____

Faith

Do you tend to see God's possibilities in difficult circumstances? _____

Are you known for your unshakable trust in God? _____

Do you maintain confidence in God despite obstacles? _____

Total for Faith: _____

Giving

Do you find joy in giving to others or to the church? _____

Are you able to give sacrificially without resentment? _____

Do you notice and meet financial needs in ministry? _____

Total for Giving: _____

Healing

Has God used you to bring physical/emotional healing to others? _____

Do you have a strong desire to see people healed? _____

Do people seek you out for prayer when they're sick? _____

Total for Healing: _____

Helps

Do you find fulfillment in helping others with practical tasks? _____

Are you often the first to notice and meet others' needs? _____

Do you enjoy supporting others behind the scenes? _____

Total for Helps: _____

Hospitality

Do you enjoy making others feel comfortable and at home? _____

Is your home often open to guests? _____

Do others comment on feeling welcome in your presence? _____

Total for Hospitality: _____

SPIRITUAL GIFTS ASSESSMENT QUESTIONS

Intercession

Do you spend significant time in prayer for others? _____

Do you often feel led by the Spirit to pray for specific needs? _____

Do you see clear answers to your prayers for others? _____

Total for Intercession: _____

Knowledge

Do you have a hunger for studying and understanding Scripture? _____

Can you explain difficult concepts in ways others can understand? _____

Do others seek your understanding of biblical concepts? _____

Total for Knowledge: _____

Leadership

Do others naturally look to you for direction? _____

Are you able to cast vision and motivate others towards a goal? _____

Do you see ways to help others achieve shared goals? _____

Total for Leadership: _____

Mercy

Are you drawn to help those who are hurting? _____

Do you find it easy to forgive and show compassion to others? _____

Are you quickly moved to assist those in distress? _____

Total for Mercy: _____

Miracles

Have you witnessed God perform miracles through your prayers? _____

Do you have faith for the seemingly impossible? _____

Do you regularly pray expecting supernatural intervention? _____

Total for Miracles: _____

Pastoring/Shepherding

Do you feel a calling to nurture others' spiritual growth? _____

Are you patient in guiding others through their spiritual journey? _____

Do people seek your spiritual guidance regularly? _____

Total for Pastoring/Shepherding: _____

SPIRITUAL GIFTS ASSESSMENT QUESTIONS

Prophecy

Do you often feel God giving you messages for others? ____

Are you compelled to speak truth, even when it's difficult? ____

Do your words bring conviction or revelation to others? ____

Total for Prophecy: ____

Service

Do you find joy in behind-the-scenes work? ____

Are you always looking for ways to help out? ____

Do you prefer serving others to being served? ____

Total for Service: ____

Teaching

Do you enjoy studying and sharing biblical insights? ____

Can you explain Scripture in ways that help others apply it to their lives? ____

Do others say they learn from your teaching? ____

Total for Teaching: ____

Tongues

Have you experienced speaking in an unknown language during prayer? ____

Do you feel led to pray in tongues regularly? ____

Are you comfortable using this gift in appropriate settings? ____

Total for Tongues: ____

Interpretation

Do you sometimes understand messages given in unknown tongues? ____

Do others confirm the accuracy of your interpretations? ____

Do you receive interpretation of tongues during corporate worship? ____

Total for Interpretation: ____

Wisdom

Do people seek your advice for complex life issues? ____

Can you often see Godly solutions to difficult problems? ____

Do you effectively apply spiritual truth to specific situations? ____

Total for Wisdom: ____

Spiritual Gifts

YOUR TOP SPIRITUAL GIFTS	HIGHEST SCORES
_____	Score: _____
_____	Score: _____
_____	Score: _____
_____	Score: _____
_____	Score: _____

"God's dream for your life is bigger *than the dream you have for yourself.*"

T.D. Jakes

CHAPTER 18

Discovering Your Unique Calling

PERSONAL REFLECTION QUESTIONS

Prayerfully reflect on these questions to discover how God has uniquely designed you for His Kingdom. By building on your spiritual gifts, your responses will reveal how your passions, and life experiences point to your unique calling and distinctive purpose in God's plan.

Life Experiences

What significant events have shaped you? When have you felt most aligned with God's will?

What childhood dreams or aspirations have continued into adulthood?

Passions & Interests

What activities or causes ignite your heart? What injustices stir you to action?

If you had unlimited resources, what specific need would you address first?

Talents & Abilities

What strengths come naturally to you? Where do others often seek your help?

What consistent affirmations have you received regarding your abilities?

Spiritual Connection

When do you feel most connected to God? What patterns emerge from your answers?

Where do your abilities and spiritual gifts intersect with the needs that move you?

Divine Direction

What doors has God been opening for you? How do you envision serving God in the most fulfilling way?

What opportunities do you have to use your gifts in service to God and others?

✧ ✧ ✧

"When you discover your divine purpose, fear loses its grip and God-fidence takes its place—*you finally understand the anchored truth of whose you are and why you were created.*"

Sharri Burggraaf
Women of Purpose

✧ ✧ ✧

YOUR DIVINE APPOINTMENT

We've now reached the section you've been waiting for—the very heart of why this book was written. Throughout these pages we've explored the shared God-given purpose for every believer: to know God through Jesus Christ and to make Him known through discipleship. This is a holy encounter—a sacred moment of divine revelation. You now stand on the brink of discovering the unique and beautiful calling God has intricately woven into the fabric of your being since before time began. Your entire life has led you to this moment of revelation and purpose.

Through this journey, you've courageously faced your fears, exposed the lies that once held you captive, and immersed yourself in transformative truths. Each step has been purposeful, each revelation significant. Like a master artisan preparing a canvas, God has been readying your heart and mind for this pivotal unveiling. The specific calling God has for your life is as unique as your fingerprint.

At the moment of your salvation, you began building your life on the unshakeable foundation of Jesus Christ. As **1 Corinthians 3:11** affirms, *"For no one can lay any foundation other than the one already laid, which is Jesus Christ."* All the truths you've embraced, the hard work you've done, and the growth you've experienced throughout this study have been preparing the sturdy framework upon which your life's purpose will now be built. Perhaps you're already walking in part of what God has called you to do. If so, that's wonderful! This process isn't about starting from scratch, but about refining and expanding your understanding of God's purpose for your life.

Our purpose often unfolds in layers. What you're doing now may be just the beginning of a grander vision God has prepared for you. This process can help you see the bigger picture, connect the dots between current activities and future possibilities, and step more fully into the abundant life God has already prepared for you. The God who called you *"is faithful, and He will do it".* **1 Thessalonians 5:24**

Approach this moment with prayer, expectant faith, open hands; and a willing heart.

Ephesians 2:10

We are God's Handiwork

"For we are God's handiwork, created in Christ Jesus to do good works, which God prepared in advance for us to do."

190

FORMULATING YOUR PURPOSE STATEMENT

Through prayerful consideration and reflection, discover the unique tapestry God has woven, reflecting your identity in Christ, spiritual gifts, talents, and experiences. Whether God's calling you to faithful service in everyday moments or expansive ministry leadership, celebrate the distinctive design He's created in you. This guide will help you clearly articulate your divine calling with clarity and conviction.

Key Elements to Include

- Identity in Christ: Acknowledge who you are as God's beloved child
- Current Journey: Reflect your present spiritual season
- Gifts and Talents: Highlight your unique abilities and experiences
- Action and Intention: Describe how you will serve
- Target Group or Outcome: Specify the impact you aim to make
- Divine Guidance: Leave room for God's ongoing leadership

Purpose Statement Formula

Use the following flexible template to craft your purpose statement:

"I am _____ [identity in Christ], _____ [current state or journey], using my _____ [gifts/talents/experiences] to _____[action verb] _____[target group/cause/outcome] as God leads me."

Guiding Principles

- Your purpose statement is not a one-time declaration, but a living document that can change as God reveals your calling more fully.
- It should align with Scripture and resonate with your heart.
- Regularly revisit it and remain open to God's gentle guidance.
- Focus on advancing God's Kingdom through your unique design.
- Callings come in all sizes; from quiet, consistent acts of service to large-scale ministries. Both are equally valuable in advancing God's Kingdom and perfectly suited to your unique spiritual gifts and how He's designed you to serve.

Remember

Your purpose and unique calling is both a gift and a responsibility from God. It can be daily faithfulness in small but eternally significant acts or an expansive ministry platform; both are perfectly tailored to who God created you to be. As **Jeremiah 29:11** promises, "'*For I know the plans I have for you,' declares the Lord, 'plans to prosper you and not to harm you, to give you hope and a future.*'" Trust that His plans for you are good, and specifically fashioned for your unique combination of gifts, experiences, talents and passions. As you grow and mature in Christ, your understanding may deepen and expand.

My Purpose

_____

_____

_____

_____

_____

_____

_____

_____

_____

_____

_____

CHAPTER 19

Living Out Your Purpose

LEAVING THE WOMAN OF YOUR PAST BEHIND

"Do not call to mind the former things or consider things of the past. Behold I am going to do something new. Now it will spring up; will you not be aware of it?" **Isaiah 43:18-19**

You are a child of God, a daughter of the King. This identity transcends any label the world might have placed on you or any narrative you may have believed about yourself.

This begins with a simple yet powerful truth: you are not defined by your past. Your past, whether marked by trauma, mistakes, challenges, or unfulfilled potential—does not define you or limit your future potential or purpose. Your path and purpose is determined by God.

You are a new creation in Christ. The old has gone; the new has come! God is doing something entirely new in you. While past experiences have shaped you, they do not dictate or limit what God can do in you and through you. He redeems our deepest wounds and transforms them into a powerful ministry. Your Heavenly Father sees beyond who you've been and what has happened to you, to who He created you to be. You're invited to shed the layers of your old self and emerge into the fullness of who God created you to be, walking out all He has for you that is already yours!

As you step into the fullness of your divine calling, remember:
- Your true identity is secure in Christ Jesus
- Your past is redeemed for God's purposes
- You stand as an overcomer through Christ
- You can walk in the freedom Jesus secured for you

While this book's focus in not primarily on healing, Jesus Christ is your SOUL HEALER, and your purpose flows from your healed identity in Him. Replace any lingering lies with God's truth with your unique truth arsenal and fully embrace the truth that the woman He sees when He looks at you—is beautiful, capable, and purposeful beyond measure. It's time to align your vision with His and step into the extraordinary life He has prepared for you.

Embracing Your Divine Design and Sacred Purpose

Now that you've released the woman of your past, it's time to fully embrace who God created you to be. Living as a woman of purpose means walking out your identity in Christ Jesus. You are healed. You are an overcomer. You are more than a conqueror and you can step into the victory and freedom that was won through Jesus Christ. Jesus won the victory so you are victorious.

In the sacred truth of Scripture, we find the profound reality that you are created in God's image, reflecting His divine nature and character. This foundational concept affirms your inherent dignity and worth as a daughter of God, highlighting your unique role in bearing the likeness of your Creator. As we explore the divine narrative of redemption, we unveil a powerful truth: you, liberated by God's grace, are entrusted with a sacred calling to fulfill His purposes.

At the heart of every godly woman lies a significant truth: you are not merely a passive observer, but a dynamic force of action. Like the woman in Proverbs 31, you skillfully navigate the complexities of your roles—nurturing relationships, managing responsibilities, using your talents, and serving your community. You embody the essence of both servant and leader, gracefully balancing multiple responsibilities. Yet, amidst the whirlwind of life, you are called to a sacred pause— a gentle reminder that your foremost relationship is with your Creator. You are invited to cultivate a deep, intimate relationship with Jesus, infusing His character into the very fabric of your being.

In a world where societal norms often mislead women in their search for purpose, this journey offers you transformation through rediscovering your true calling. As you immerse yourself in God's Word, He will reveal Himself in gentle whispers, speaking directly to your heart. Your purpose isn't just an intellectual exercise—it's a sacred covenant between you and God to steward the calling He has entrusted to you in intimacy with Him, the lover of your soul. When you understand your divine design, you're compelled to align your life with Him, making intentional choices that honor your calling. Your purpose declaration becomes both your anchor in difficult times and your compass for daily decisions. Embrace this journey of self-discovery as you draw closer to God's heart. As you seek God, not just to find your purpose and unique calling, you'll feel compelled to declare your commitment to Him, stepping into the fullness of all God has created you to be as you live it out.

A WOMAN OF PURPOSE DECLARATION

As a woman of purpose, I proclaim these words over my life, aligning myself with God's will and His Word. Integrity and honesty protect me, for I put my hope in You, Lord. I will do what is right and just as I live an intentional, Spirit-filled life, acting with love, justice, mercy, and humility, relying on God in all things. I am a woman of purpose, nobility, tenacity, empathy, compassion, grace, strength, resilience, and trustworthiness, yielding to the Lord. I commit to embody the characteristics of biblical femininity, valuing myself as God's creation and celebrating others. I will devote myself fully to Christ, allowing His Word to define my life and guide my priorities. I am a woman of worth, value, consistency, and stability in all my actions, thoughts, and beliefs. I am upright and outstanding, and because of Jesus, I am unstoppable. I wasn't born to be a worrier; I am a warrior and I was called to be brave, bold, and courageous. I have the ability to maintain ethical standards without compromising my values, morals, and principles in all situations. I am truthful, honest, sincere, and I possess a sense of honor, reliability, and accountability to God my Creator and my Lord and Savior Jesus Christ.

I resolve to extend kindness, patience, and forgiveness to others, making amends where necessary, forgiving those who have wronged me and seek reconciliation where I have wronged others. I will esteem others with my time, concern, and full attention, releasing them from the prison of my hurt and anger. I will strive to live with the highest standards of virtue and purity, being a blessing to those around me. I will nurture and train my children in righteousness, making my home a welcoming and loving place and resolve to leave a godly spiritual legacy.. I will work diligently to provide for the needs of my family and those entrusted to my care.

I will honor the sanctity of life, valuing and protecting every life as precious in God's sight. I will stand for life, from conception to natural death, defending and advocating for the innocent. I resolve to have my words encourage and build up rather than tear down. I speak up for myself, set boundaries, and speak for those who can't yet speak for themselves. Let God weigh me on the scales of justice, for He knows that I am a woman of elegance and excellence for His glory.

I will live today with tomorrow in mind, honoring God in all my actions and decisions. I will confront evil, pursue justice, and love mercy, standing firm in my faith. I will pray for others, treating them with kindness, respect, and compassion. I will learn from my mistakes, repent of my sins, and walk as a woman answerable to God. I honor God with my life as a living sacrifice, secure and defined by the identity of Christ, living authentically, surprisingly satisfied, and faithfully His, joyfully honoring God as a purposefully feminine woman and sister in Christ, resolving to live with grace and dignity.

I will seek to honor God, be faithful, obey His Word, and do His will, courageously working with the strength He provides to fulfill this resolution for the rest of my life for His glory.

CELEBRATING YOUR PURPOSE

Congratulations, beloved! You have articulated your God-given purpose—a moment of profound significance in your walk with Christ. This is not merely the end of an exercise, but the beginning of a new chapter in your spiritual journey. Let's take time to reflect on and celebrate this beautiful revelation.

The Significance of Your Purpose

The purpose and calling you've uncovered is a testament to God's unique design for your life. It represents the intersection of your gifts, passions, and the specific way God intends to use you for His glory and the advancement of His Kingdom. This purpose is both a blessing and a responsibility—a calling to steward well the divine assignment you've been given. The revelation of your God-given purpose is cause for great celebration! As you uncover the specific ways God has designed you to impact His Kingdom, we encourage you to mark this moment with joy and reverence. Here are some ways to celebrate this spiritual milestone:

Worship and Thanksgiving: Spend time in heartfelt worship, thanking God for His faithfulness in bringing you to this point of clarity and purpose.

Sacred Declaration: Write out your purpose statement and read it aloud as a declaration over your life. Consider inviting close friends or family to witness this powerful moment.

Symbolic Act: Plant a tree, light a candle, or choose another meaningful symbol to represent the new growth and the light your purpose will bring to the world.

Community Sharing: Share your purpose with your small group or trusted spiritual mentors. Allow them to pray over you and affirm the calling God has placed on your life.

Dedicatory Prayer: Offer a prayer of dedication, surrendering your newfound purpose to God and asking for His guidance and empowerment to live it out.

Create a Visual Reminder: Design a piece of art, write a poem, or create a vision board that represents your purpose. Display it prominently as a daily reminder of God's call on your life.

Acts of Service: Begin living out your purpose immediately by planning a specific act of service aligned with your newly articulated calling.

Jeremiah 29:11

Plans to Give You a Hope

"*For I know the plans I have for you, declares the Lord, plans to prosper you and not to harm you, plans to give you hope and a future.*"

197

MOVING FORWARD IN PURPOSE

As you step into this new season of purposeful living, remember that your journey of discovery and growth is ongoing. Your purpose may evolve and deepen as you walk closely with God, but its foundation, rooted in His love and design for you—remains unwavering. Let your newly articulated purpose serve as a guiding light, shaping your decisions, influencing your priorities, and inspiring you to live each day with intention and passion. As you do, trust in the promise of **Philippians 1:6**: *"Being confident of this, that He who began a good work in you will carry it on to completion until the day of Christ Jesus."* When God calls us to something, He equips us and fulfills the work He has entrusted to us. Walk forward with confidence, knowing that you are seen, known, and purposefully created by the God of the universe for a specific reason. You are His delight. As you delight in the Lord and live out your calling, you bring glory to His name and light to the world around you.

Embrace your purpose with unwavering conviction. Live it boldly, fueled by the joy of knowing you are fulfilling the divine calling for which you were fearfully and wonderfully created. Step forward with confidence, for you are walking the path lovingly crafted for you by the Creator of the universe—your Creator!

May your life shine as a radiant testament to the transformative power of Jesus Christ, inspiring others to discover their own God-given purpose. You are a Woman of Purpose— uniquely designed, divinely called, and empowered by the Holy Spirit to make an eternal impact for the Kingdom of God. Now go forth and let your light shine!

Philippians 1:6

Will Carry it to Completion

"Being confident of this, that He who began a good work in you will carry it on to completion until the day of Christ Jesus."

Closing Reflections and Prayer From the Author

My beloved sisters in Christ,

My heart overflows with prayers and hopes for your journey ahead. I pray that you walk confidently in the victory Jesus Christ has already secured for you, fully embracing our shared identity as believers; to know God intimately through Jesus Christ and to make Him known through transformative discipleship. Throughout this study, your life has been lifted before the throne of grace in prayer, asking the Lord to surround you with His protection, illuminate your path with His wisdom, and ignite you with Holy Spirit boldness as He unveils the unique calling He has authored specifically for you.

From my heart to yours, I want to offer both gentle preparation and celebration. This sacred journey we're traveling together is breathtakingly beautiful and life-altering, yet it demands courage for the real challenges that lie ahead. There will be seasons when living out these declarations feels like walking uphill, when unexpected obstacles emerge, and when trials test the very foundation of your resolve. In those defining moments, remember that these challenges aren't evidence of failure, and they don't take away from the commitment you've made in this chapter of your life. They are God's invitations to experience His sufficiency and deepen your dependence and reliance on God in ways that will astound you as you surrender completely to Him. When obstacles come—and they will, He will create opportunities for His Son Jesus to shine through you. Our adversary will indeed probe our vulnerable places, but even there, we discover that His grace is not only enough, it is extravagant, His strength not merely adequate, it is overwhelming, and His faithfulness not just reliable, it is unshakeable.

When the weight feels unbearable, when whispers of doubt crescendo, when everything seems beyond your capacity, that is precisely when you step into the sacred space where God's power meets your surrender. Here you will find that He who lives within you is infinitely greater than any force that opposes you, that the One who has called you is eternally faithful, and that He delights in equipping you for every good work He has lovingly prepared for your hands.

You are never walking alone. Jesus walks beside you, the Holy Spirit empowers you, and the Father who orchestrated your calling will complete what He has begun. As you step forward into your divine purpose, I am filled with holy anticipation, knowing that God will use your unique gifts, your redeemed story, and your surrendered heart to bring His Kingdom to earth in ways only you can. You have been called for such a time as this, beloved, and I cannot wait to witness the extraordinary ways God will move through your obedient "yes."

Sharri Burggraaf

MY AFFIRMATIONS

Appendix
Resources for Additional Study

APPENDIX A: GOING DEEPER

OUR IDENTITY IN CHRIST: COMPLETE SCRIPTURE REFERENCES

Chosen: Ephesians 1:4 - *"just as He chose us in Him before the foundation of the world, that we should be holy and without blame before Him in love,"*

Holy and Blameless: Ephesians 1:4 - *"just as He chose us in Him before the foundation of the world, that we should be holy and without blame before Him in love,"*

Predestined: Ephesians 1:5 - *"having predestined us to adoption as sons by Jesus Christ to Himself, according to the good pleasure of His will,"*

Adopted: Ephesians 1:5 - *"having predestined us to adoption as sons by Jesus Christ to Himself, according to the good pleasure of His will,"*

Accepted: Ephesians 1:6 - *"to the praise of the glory of His grace, by which He made us accepted in the Beloved."*

Beloved: Ephesians 1:6 - *"to the praise of the glory of His grace, by which He made us accepted in the Beloved."*

Redeemed: Ephesians 1:7 - *"In Him we have redemption through His blood, the forgiveness of sins, according to the riches of His grace"*

Forgiven: Ephesians 1:7 - *"In Him we have redemption through His blood, the forgiveness of sins, according to the riches of His grace"*

Heirs of the inheritance: Ephesians 1:11 - *"In Him also we have obtained an inheritance, being predestined according to the purpose of Him who works all things according to the counsel of His will,"*

Saved: Ephesians 1:13 - *"In Him you also trusted, after you heard the word of truth, the gospel of your salvation; in whom also, having believed, you were sealed with the Holy Spirit of promise,"*

Sealed with the Holy Spirit: Ephesians 1:13 - *"In Him you also trusted, after you heard the word of truth, the gospel of your salvation; in whom also, having believed, you were sealed with the Holy Spirit of promise,"*

Other Bible verses that tell us our identity:

Children of God: John 1:12 *"But to all who did receive him, who believed in His name, He gave the right to become children of God."*

Romans 8:16 - *"The Spirit himself bears witness with our spirit that we are children of God,"*

Heir of God Co-heirs with Christ: Romans 8:17 *"Now if we are children, then we are heirs—heirs of God and co-heirs with Christ, if indeed we share in his sufferings in order that we may also share in his glory."*

APPENDIX A: GOING DEEPER

OUR IDENTITY IN CHRIST: COMPLETE SCRIPTURE REFERENCES (CONTINUED)

Citizens of Heaven: Philippians 3:20-21 *"But our citizenship is in heaven. And we eagerly await a Savior from there, the Lord Jesus Christ, who, by the power that enables him to bring everything under his control, will transform our lowly bodies so that they will be like his glorious body."*

A Royal Priesthood: 1 Peter 2:9 *"But you are a chosen people, a royal priesthood, a holy nation, God's special possession, that you may declare the praises of him who called you out of darkness into his wonderful light."*

New Creations: 2 Corinthians 5:17 *"Therefore, if anyone is in Christ, the new creation has come: The old has gone, the new is here!"*

Joint-heirs with Christ: Romans 8:17 *"Now if we are children, then we are heirs—heirs of God and co-heirs with Christ, if indeed we share in his sufferings in order that we may also share in his glory."*

Chosen and Holy: Colossians 3:12 - *"Put on then, as God's chosen ones, holy and beloved, compassionate hearts, kindness, humility, meekness, and patience,"*

Set Apart: 1 Peter 2:9 - *"But you are a chosen race, a royal priesthood, a holy nation, a people for his own possession, that you may proclaim the excellencies of him who called you out of darkness into his marvelous light."*

God's Workmanship: Ephesians 2:10 - *"For we are his workmanship, created in Christ Jesus for good works, which God prepared beforehand, that we should walk in them."*

Partakers of the Divine Nature: 2 Peter 1:4 - *"by which he has granted to us his precious and very great promises, so that through them you may become partakers of the divine nature, having escaped from the corruption that is in the world because of sinful desire."*

Called to His Kingdom and Glory: 1 Thessalonians 2:12 - *"we exhorted each one of you and encouraged you and charged you to walk in a manner worthy of God, who calls you into his own kingdom and glory."*

God's Temple: 1 Corinthians 3:16 - *"Do you not know that you are God's temple and that God's Spirit dwells in you?"*

John 1:12 - "But to all who did receive him, who believed in his name, he gave the right to become children of God,"

Romans 8:15 - "For you did not receive the spirit of slavery to fall back into fear, but you have received the Spirit of adoption as sons, by whom we cry, 'Abba! Father!'"

John 3:1 - "See what kind of love the Father has given to us, that we should be called children of God; and so we are. The reason why the world does not know us is that it did not know him."

APPENDIX A: GOING DEEPER

Song of Solomon 6:3 - *"I am my beloved's and my beloved is mine; he grazes among the lilies."*

Ambassadors for Christ: 2 Corinthians 5:20 - *"We are therefore Christ's ambassadors, as though God were making his appeal through us."*

Branch of the True Vine: John 15:5 - *"I am the vine; you are the branches. If you remain in me and I in you, you will bear much fruit."*

Fearfully and Wonderfully Made: Psalm 139:14 - *"I praise you because I am fearfully and wonderfully made; your works are wonderful, I know that full well."*

Friend of God: John 15:15 - *"I no longer call you servants, because a servant does not know his master's business. Instead, I have called you friends."*

Hidden with Christ in God: Colossians 3:3 - *"For you died, and your life is now hidden with Christ in God."*

Light of the World: Matthew 5:14 - *"You are the light of the world. A town built on a hill cannot be hidden."*

More Than Conquerors: Romans 8:37 - *"In all these things we are more than conquerors through him who loved us."*

Overcomers: 1 John 5:4 - *"For everyone born of God overcomes the world. This is the victory that has overcome the world, even our faith."*

Salt of the Earth: Matthew 5:13 - *"You are the salt of the earth."*

Saints: Ephesians 1:1 - *"To the saints in Ephesus, the faithful in Christ Jesus."*

Victorious: 1 Corinthians 15:57 - *"But thanks be to God! He gives us the victory through our Lord Jesus Christ."*

APPENDIX B : BIBLICAL TRUTHS TO COUNTER COMMON LIES

I'm Inherently Good

The following powerful bible verses dispel the lie that I am bad. God emphasizes the goodness of His creation. God created mankind in His image. After everything God created He always said "It was good". When God created mankind He said *"it was very good."* As a result, I am inherently good in God's eyes.

Genesis 1:26-27 - *"Then God said, 'Let us make man in our image, after our likeness. And let them have dominion over the fish of the sea and over the birds of the heavens and over the livestock and over all the earth and over every creeping thing that creeps on the earth.' So God created man in his own image, in the image of God He created him; male and female He created them."*

Genesis 1:31 *"And God saw everything that He had made, and behold, it was very good. And there was evening and there was morning, the sixth day."*

Genesis 2:7 - *"then the Lord God formed the man of dust from the ground and breathed into his nostrils the breath of life, and the man became a living creature."*

Psalm 139:14: *"I praise you, for I am fearfully and wonderfully made. Wonderful are your works; my soul knows it very well."*

Ephesians 2:10: *"For we are his workmanship, created in Christ Jesus for good works, which God prepared beforehand, that we should walk in them."*

Ephesians 1:4: *"Even as He chose us in him before the foundation of the world, that we should be holy and blameless before Him. in love."*

Romans 8:1: *"There is therefore now no condemnation for those who are in Christ Jesus."*

1 Timothy 4:4 - *"For everything created by God is good, and nothing is to be rejected if it is received with thanksgiving,"*

APPENDIX B: BIBLICAL TRUTHS TO COUNTER COMMON LIES
I Have Much Worth

The following powerful bible verses dispel the lie that I am worthless. God places significance on mankind who are created in His image. Despite human imperfection and sin, God's love and grace are extended to all, underscoring each person's worth in His eyes. Humans reflect aspects of God's character and nature, imbuing them with inherent dignity and worth.

Psalm 139:13-14 - *"For you formed my inward parts; you knitted me together in my mother's womb. I praise you, for I am fearfully and wonderfully made. Wonderful are your works; my soul knows it very well."*

Ephesians 2:10 - *"For we are his workmanship, created in Christ Jesus for good works, which God prepared beforehand, that we should walk in them."*

Isaiah 43:4 - *"Because you are precious in my eyes, and honored, and I love you, I give men in return for you, peoples in exchange for your life."*

1 Peter 2:9 - *"But you are a chosen race, a royal priesthood, a holy nation, a people for His own possession, that you may proclaim the excellencies of Him who called you out of darkness into His marvelous light."*

Matthew 10:29-31 - *"Are not two sparrows sold for a penny? And not one of them will fall to the ground apart from your Father. But even the hairs of your head are all numbered. Fear not, therefore; you are of more value than many sparrows."*

Luke 12:6-7 - *"Are not five sparrows sold for two pennies? And not one of them is forgotten before God. Why, even the hairs of your head are all numbered. Fear not; you are of more value than many sparrows."*

1 Corinthians 6:19-20 - *"Or do you not know that your body is a temple of the Holy Spirit within you, whom you have from God? You are not your own, for you were bought with a price. So glorify God in your body."*

APPENDIX B: BIBLICAL TRUTHS TO COUNTER COMMON LIES

I'm Unconditionally Loved

The following powerful bible verses dispel the lie that I am unlovable.

John 3:16 *"For God so loved the world, that he gave His only begotten Son, that whoever believes in Him should not perish but have eternal life."*

1 John 4:8 *"Anyone who does not love does not know God, because God is love."*

Jeremiah 31:3 - *"The Lord appeared to him from far away. I have loved you with an everlasting love; therefore I have continued my faithfulness to you."*

1 John 3:1 - *"See what kind of love the Father has given to us, that we should be called children of God; and so we are."*

Zephaniah 3:17 - *"The Lord your God is in your midst, a mighty one who will save; He will rejoice over you with gladness; He will quiet you by His love; He will exult over you with loud singing."*

John 15:9 - *"As the Father has loved me, so have I loved you. Abide in My love."*

Ephesians 2:4-5 - *"But God, being rich in mercy, because of the great love with which He loved us, even when we were dead in our trespasses, made us alive together with Christ—by grace you have been saved—"*

Romans 5:8 - *"But God shows his love for us in that while we were still sinners, Christ died for us."*

1 John 4:9-10 - *"In this the love of God was made manifest among us, that God sent His only Son into the world, so that we might live through him. In this is love, not that we have loved God but that He loved us and sent His Son to be the propitiation for our sins."*

Psalm 86:15 - *"But you, O Lord, are a God merciful and gracious, slow to anger and abounding in steadfast love and faithfulness."*

Psalm 136:26 - *"Give thanks to the God of heaven, for his steadfast love endures forever."*

Lamentations 3:22-23 - *"The steadfast love of the Lord never ceases; His mercies never come to an end; they are new every morning;*

APPENDIX B: BIBLICAL TRUTHS TO COUNTER COMMON LIES
I'm Wanted & Chosen

The following powerful bible verses dispel the lie that I am unwanted.

Jeremiah 31:3 - *"The Lord appeared to him from far away. I have loved you with an everlasting love; therefore I have continued my faithfulness to you."*

1 John 3:1 - *"See what kind of love the Father has given to us, that we should be called children of God; and so we are."*

Zephaniah 3:17 - *"The Lord your God is in your midst, a mighty one who will save; he will rejoice over you with gladness; he will quiet you by his love; he will exult over you with loud singing."*

John 15:9 - *"As the Father has loved me, so have I loved you. Abide in my love."*

saiah 43:1 - *"But now thus says the Lord, He who created you, O Jacob, He who formed you, O Israel: 'Fear not, for I have redeemed you; I have called you by name, you are Mine.'"*

Psalm 139:17-18 - *"How precious to me are your thoughts, O God! How vast is the sum of them! If I would count them, they are more than the sand. I awake, and I am still with you."*

Ephesians 1:4-5 - *"even as he chose us in him before the foundation of the world, that we should be holy and blameless before Him. In love He predestined us for adoption to Himself as sons through Jesus Christ, according to the purpose of His will,"*

1 Peter 2:9 - *"But you are a chosen race, a royal priesthood, a holy nation, a people for his own possession, that you may proclaim the excellencies of him who called you out of darkness into his marvelous light."*

Romans 5:8 - *"but God shows his love for us in that while we were still sinners, Christ died for us."*

John 14:18 - *"I will not leave you as orphans; I will come to you."*

APPENDIX B: BIBLICAL TRUTHS TO COUNTER COMMON LIES

God Will Protect Me

The following powerful bible verses dispel the lie that I have to protect myself because God won't protect me.

Psalm 91:2: *"I will say to the Lord, 'My refuge and my fortress, my God, in whom I trust."*

Isaiah 41:10: *"Fear not, for I am with you; be not dismayed, for I am your God; I will strengthen you, I will help you, I will uphold you with my righteous right hand."*

Psalm 18:2: *"The Lord is my rock and my fortress and my deliverer, my God, my rock, in whom I take refuge, my shield, and the horn of my salvation, my stronghold."*

Psalm 91:4-6: *"He will cover you with his pinions, and under His wings you will find refuge; His faithfulness is a shield and buckler. You will not fear the terror of the night, nor the arrow that flies by day, nor the pestilence that stalks in darkness, nor the destruction that wastes at noonday."*

Isaiah 41:10: *"Fear not, for I am with you; be not dismayed, for I am your God; I will strengthen you, I will help you, I will uphold you with my righteous right hand."*

Isaiah 43:2: *"When you pass through the waters, I will be with you; and through the rivers, they shall not overwhelm you; when you walk through fire you shall not be burned, and the flame shall not consume you."*

2 Thessalonians 3:3 - *"But the Lord is faithful. He will establish you and guard you against the evil one."*

Psalm 46:1 - *"God is our refuge and strength, a very present help in trouble."*

Proverbs 18:10 - *"The name of the Lord is a strong tower; the righteous man runs into it and is safe."*

Psalm 121:7-8 - *"The Lord will keep you from all evil; He will keep your life. The Lord will keep your going out and your coming in from this time forth and forevermore."*

APPENDIX B: BIBLICAL TRUTHS TO COUNTER COMMON LIES
I'm Never Alone

The following powerful bible verses dispel the lie that I am alone or abandoned.

Deuteronomy 31:6 - *"Be strong and courageous. Do not fear or be in dread of them, for it is the Lord your God who goes with you. He will not leave you or forsake you."*

Isaiah 41:10 - *"Fear not, for I am with you; be not dismayed, for I am your God; I will strengthen you, I will help you, I will uphold you with my righteous right hand."*

Matthew 28:20 - *"Teaching them to observe all that I have commanded you. And behold, I am with you always, to the end of the age."*

Psalm 23:4 - *"Even though I walk through the valley of the shadow of death, I will fear no evil, for you are with me; your rod and your staff, they comfort me."*

Hebrews 13:5 - *"Keep your life free from love of money, and be content with what you have, for he has said, 'I will never leave you nor forsake you.'"*

Joshua 1:9 - *"Have I not commanded you? Be strong and courageous. Do not be frightened, and do not be dismayed, for the Lord your God is with you wherever you go."*

John 14:18 - *"I will not leave you as orphans; I will come to you."*

Isaiah 43:2 - *"When you pass through the waters, I will be with you; and through the rivers, they shall not overwhelm you; when you walk through fire you shall not be burned, and the flame shall not consume you."*

Psalm 27:10 - *"For my father and my mother have forsaken me, but the Lord will take me in."*

1 Kings 8:57 - *"The Lord our God be with us, as he was with our fathers. May he not leave us or forsake us."*

Isaiah 49:15-16 - *"'Can a woman forget her nursing child, that she should have no compassion on the son of her womb? Even these may forget, yet I will not forget you."*

APPENDIX B: BIBLICAL TRUTHS TO COUNTER COMMON LIES

God Promises Healing

The following powerful bible verses dispel the lie that I am never going to heal.

Jeremiah 30:17 - *"For I will restore health to you, and your wounds I will heal, declares the Lord, because they have called you an outcast: 'It is Zion, for whom no one cares!'"*

Psalm 147:3 - *"He heals the brokenhearted and binds up their wounds."*

Isaiah 57:18-19 - *"I have seen his ways, but I will heal him; I will lead him and restore comfort to him and his mourners, creating the fruit of the lips. Peace, peace, to the far and to the near, says the Lord, and I will heal him."*

1 Peter 2:24 - *"He himself bore our sins in His body on the tree, that we might die to sin and live to righteousness. By His wounds you have been healed."*

James 5:14-15 - *"Is anyone among you sick? Let him call for the elders of the church, and let them pray over him, anointing him with oil in the name of the Lord. And the prayer of faith will save the one who is sick, and the Lord will raise him up. And if he has committed sins, he will be forgiven."*

Psalm 103:2-4 - *"Bless the Lord, O my soul, and forget not all his benefits, who forgives all your iniquity, who heals all your diseases, who redeems your life from the pit, who crowns you with steadfast love and mercy,"*

Malachi 4:2 - *"But for you who fear my name, the sun of righteousness shall rise with healing in its wings. You shall go out leaping like calves from the stall."*

Isaiah 53:5 - *"But He was pierced for our transgressions; He was crushed for our iniquities; upon Him was the chastisement that brought us peace, and with His wounds we are healed."*

Jeremiah 33:6 - *"Behold, I will bring to it health and healing, and I will heal them and reveal to them abundance of prosperity and security."*

3 John 1:2 - *"Beloved, I pray that all may go well with you and that you may be in good health, as it goes well with your soul."*

APPENDIX B: BIBLICAL TRUTHS TO COUNTER COMMON LIES
I'm Forgiven and Redeemed

The following powerful bible verses dispel the lie that I am beyond forgiveness or redemption.

1 John 1:9 - *"If we confess our sins, he is faithful and just to forgive us our sins and to cleanse us from all unrighteousness."*

Isaiah 1:18 - *"Come now, let us reason together, says the Lord: though your sins are like scarlet, they shall be as white as snow; though they are red like crimson, they shall become like wool."*

Ephesians 1:7 - *"In him we have redemption through His blood, the forgiveness of our trespasses, according to the riches of His grace."*

Micah 7:18-19 - *"Who is a God like you, pardoning iniquity and passing over transgression for the remnant of His inheritance? He does not retain His anger forever, because He delights in steadfast love. He will again have compassion on us; He will tread our iniquities underfoot. You will cast all our sins into the depths of the sea."*

Psalm 103:12 - *"As far as the east is from the west, so far does he remove our transgressions from us."*

Romans 8:1: *"There is therefore now no condemnation for those who are in Christ Jesus."*

Romans 3:23-24 - *"For all have sinned and fall short of the glory of God, and are justified by his grace as a gift, through the redemption that is in Christ Jesus."*

Isaiah 44:22 - *"I have blotted out your transgressions like a cloud and your sins like mist; return to me, for I have redeemed you."*

Colossians 1:13-14 - *"He has delivered us from the domain of darkness and transferred us to the kingdom of his beloved Son, in whom we have redemption, the forgiveness of sins."*

Titus 2:14 - *"Who gave himself for us to redeem us from all lawlessness and to purify for Himself a people for His own possession who are zealous for good works."*

APPENDIX B: BIBLICAL TRUTHS TO COUNTER COMMON LIES

I'm an Overcomer

The following powerful bible verses dispel the lie that I am a failure. I may fail at things but I can always try again. I'm human and will not succeed at everything but I can try my best.

Philippians 4:13 - *"I can do all things through him who strengthens me."*

Jeremiah 29:11 - *"For I know the plans I have for you, declares the Lord, plans for welfare and not for evil, to give you a future and a hope."*

Proverbs 3:5-6 - *"Trust in the Lord with all your heart, and do not lean on your own understanding. In all your ways acknowledge him, and he will make straight your paths."*

2 Timothy 1:7 - *"For God gave us a spirit not of fear but of power and love and self-control."*

Romans 8:28 - *"And we know that for those who love God all things work together for good, for those who are called according to his purpose."*

Psalm 37:23-24 - *"The steps of a man are established by the Lord, when he delights in his way; though he fall, he shall not be cast headlong, for the Lord upholds his hand."*

Isaiah 41:10 - *"Fear not, for I am with you; be not dismayed, for I am your God; I will strengthen you, I will help you, I will uphold you with my righteous right hand."*

Joshua 1:9 - *"Have I not commanded you? Be strong and courageous. Do not be frightened, and do not be dismayed, for the Lord your God is with you wherever you go."*

Psalm 73:26 - *"My flesh and my heart may fail, but God is the strength of my heart and my portion forever."*

2 Corinthians 12:9-10 - *"But He said to me, 'My grace is sufficient for you, for My power is made perfect in weakness.' Therefore I will boast all the more gladly of my weaknesses, so that the power of Christ may rest upon me. For the sake of Christ, then, I am content with weaknesses, insults, hardships, persecutions, and calamities. For when I am weak, then I am strong."*

APPENDIX B: BIBLICAL TRUTHS TO COUNTER COMMON LIES
I'm Courageous

The following powerful bible verses dispel the lie that I will always be afraid.

Isaiah 41:10 - *"Fear not, for I am with you; be not dismayed, for I am your God; I will strengthen you, I will help you, I will uphold you with My righteous right hand."*

Psalm 56:3 - *"When I am afraid, I put my trust in you."*

2 Timothy 1:7 - *"For God gave us a spirit not of fear but of power and love and self-control."*

Joshua 1:9 - *"Have I not commanded you? Be strong and courageous. Do not be frightened, and do not be dismayed, for the Lord your God is with you wherever you go."*

1 John 4:18 - *"There is no fear in love, but perfect love casts out fear."*

Psalm 23:4 - *"Even though I walk through the valley of the shadow of death, I will fear no evil, for you are with me; your rod and your staff, they comfort me."*

John 14:27 - *"Peace I leave with you; My peace I give to you. Not as the world gives do I give to you. Let not your hearts be troubled, neither let them be afraid."*

Psalm 27:1 - *"The Lord is my light and my salvation; whom shall I fear? The Lord is the stronghold of my life; of whom shall I be afraid?"*

Isaiah 43:1 - *"But now thus says the Lord, He who created you, O Jacob, He who formed you, O Israel: 'Fear not, for I have redeemed you; I have called you by name, you are mine.'"*

Psalm 118:6 - *"The Lord is on my side; I will not fear. What can man do to me?"*

Romans 8:38-39 - *"For I am sure that neither death nor life, nor angels nor rulers, nor things present nor things to come, nor powers, nor height nor depth, nor anything else in all creation, will be able to separate us from the love of God in Christ Jesus our Lord."*

APPENDIX B: BIBLICAL TRUTHS TO COUNTER COMMON LIES
I Have Purpose

The following powerful bible verses dispel the lie that I have no purpose.

Jeremiah 29:11 - *"For I know the plans I have for you, declares the Lord, plans for welfare and not for evil, to give you a future and a hope."*

Ephesians 2:10 - *"For we are his workmanship, created in Christ Jesus for good works, which God prepared beforehand, that we should walk in them."*

Romans 8:28 - *"And we know that for those who love God all things work together for good, for those who are called according to his purpose."*

Philippians 1:6 - *"And I am sure of this, that he who began a good work in you will bring it to completion at the day of Jesus Christ."*

Proverbs 16:9 - *"The heart of man plans his way, but the Lord establishes his steps."*

Psalm 138:8 - *"The Lord will fulfill his purpose for me; your steadfast love, O Lord, endures forever. Do not forsake the work of your hands."*

Isaiah 46:10 - *"declaring the end from the beginning and from ancient times things not yet done, saying, 'My counsel shall stand, and I will accomplish all my purpose,'"*

Proverbs 19:21 - *"Many are the plans in the mind of a man, but it is the purpose of the Lord that will stand."*

2 Timothy 1:9 - *"who saved us and called us to a holy calling, not because of our works but because of his own purpose and grace, which he gave us in Christ Jesus before the ages began,"*

1 Peter 2:9 - *"But you are a chosen race, a royal priesthood, a holy nation, a people for his own possession, that you may proclaim the excellencies of him who called you out of darkness into his marvelous light."*

Isaiah 43:7 - *"everyone who is called by my name, whom I created for my glory, whom I formed and made."*

Jeremiah 1:5 - *"Before I formed you in the womb I knew you, and before you were born I consecrated you; I appointed you a prophet to the nations."*

APPENDIX B: BIBLICAL TRUTHS TO COUNTER COMMON LIES
I was Planned

The following powerful bible verses dispel the lie that I am a mistake.

Psalm 139:14: *"I praise you, for I am fearfully and wonderfully made. Wonderful are your works; my soul knows it very well."*

Ephesians 2:10: *"For we are his workmanship, created in Christ Jesus for good works, which God prepared beforehand, that we should walk in them."*

Ephesians 1:4: *"Even as He chose us in Him before the foundation of the world, that we should be holy and blameless before Him. In love."*

Jeremiah 1:5 - *"Before I formed you in the womb I knew you, and before you were born I consecrated you; I appointed you a prophet to the nations."*

1 Peter 2:9 - *"But you are a chosen race, a royal priesthood, a holy nation, a people for his own possession, that you may proclaim the excellencies of Him who called you out of darkness into His marvelous light."*

Isaiah 43:1 - *"But now thus says the Lord, he who created you, O Jacob, he who formed you, O Israel: 'Fear not, for I have redeemed you; I have called you by name, you are mine.'"*

John 15:16 - *"You did not choose me, but I chose you and appointed you that you should go and bear fruit and that your fruit should abide, so that whatever you ask the Father in my name, He may give it to you."*

Psalm 139:13 - *"For you formed my inward parts; you knitted me together in my mother's womb."*

Galatians 1:15 - *"But when he who had set me apart before I was born, and who called me by His grace,"*

Ephesians 1:11-12 - *"In Him we have obtained an inheritance, having been predestined according to the purpose of Him who works all things according to the counsel of His will, so that we who were the first to hope in Christ might be to the praise of his glory."*

Romans 9:25-26 - *"As indeed He says in Hosea, 'Those who were not my people I will call "my people," and her who was not beloved I will call "beloved."*

APPENDIX B: BIBLICAL TRUTHS TO COUNTER COMMON LIES
God Cares For Me

The following powerful bible verses dispel the lie that no one cares for me.

1 Peter 5:7 - *"Casting all your anxieties on him, because he cares for you."*

Psalm 27:10 - *"For my father and my mother have forsaken me, but the Lord will take me in."*

Isaiah 49:15-16 - *"Can a woman forget her nursing child, that she should have no compassion on the son of her womb? Even these may forget, yet I will not forget you. Behold, I have engraved you on the palms of my hands; your walls are continually before me."*

Matthew 6:26 - *"Look at the birds of the air: they neither sow nor reap nor gather into barns, and yet your heavenly Father feeds them. Are you not of more value than they?"*

Matthew 10:29-31 - *"Are not two sparrows sold for a penny? And not one of them will fall to the ground apart from your Father. But even the hairs of your head are all numbered. Fear not, therefore; you are of more value than many sparrows."*

Romans 8:38-39 - *"For I am sure that neither death nor life, nor angels nor rulers, nor things present nor things to come, nor powers, nor height nor depth, nor anything else in all creation, will be able to separate us from the love of God in Christ Jesus our Lord."*

Zephaniah 3:17 - *"The Lord your God is in your midst, a mighty One who will save; He will rejoice over you with gladness; He will quiet you by His love; He will exult over you with loud singing."*

Isaiah 41:10 - *"Fear not, for I am with you; be not dismayed, for I am your God; I will strengthen you, I will help you, I will uphold you with my righteous right hand."*

Psalm 34:18 - *"The Lord is near to the brokenhearted and saves the crushed in spirit."*

Psalm 139:17-18 - *"How precious to me are your thoughts, O God! How vast is the sum of them! If I would count them, they are more than the sand..."*

APPENDIX B: BIBLICAL TRUTHS TO COUNTER COMMON LIES
I Can Trust God

The following powerful bible verses dispel the lie that I can't trust anyone.

Proverbs 3:5-6 - *"Trust in the Lord with all your heart, and do not lean on your own understanding. In all your ways acknowledge him, and he will make straight your paths."*

Psalm 118:8 - *"It is better to take refuge in the Lord than to trust in man."*

Jeremiah 17:7-8 - *"Blessed is the man who trusts in the Lord, whose trust is the Lord. He is like a tree planted by water, that sends out its roots by the stream, and does not fear when heat comes, for its leaves remain green, and is not anxious in the year of drought, for it does not cease to bear fruit."*

Isaiah 12:2 - *"Behold, God is my salvation; I will trust, and will not be afraid; for the Lord God is my strength and my song, and He has become my salvation."*

Psalm 56:3-4 - *"When I am afraid, I put my trust in you. In God, whose word I praise, in God I trust; I shall not be afraid. What can flesh do to me?"*

Proverbs 29:25 - *"The fear of man lays a snare, but whoever trusts in the Lord is safe."*

Psalm 62:8 - *"Trust in Him at all times, O people; pour out your heart before Him; God is a refuge for us."*

Psalm 40:4 - *"Blessed is the man who makes the Lord his trust, who does not turn to the proud, to those who go astray after a lie!"*

Isaiah 26:3-4 - *"You keep him in perfect peace whose mind is stayed on you, because he trusts in you. Trust in the Lord forever, for the Lord God is an everlasting rock."*

Psalm 9:10 - *"And those who know your name put their trust in you, for you, O Lord, have not forsaken those who seek you."*

Psalm 20:7 - *"Some trust in chariots and some in horses, but we trust in the name of the Lord our God."*

Isaiah 26:3 - *"You keep him in perfect peace whose mind is stayed on you, because he trusts in you."*

APPENDIX B: BIBLICAL TRUTHS TO COUNTER COMMON LIES
I Can Find Joy & Happiness

The following powerful bible verses dispel the lie that I will never be happy.

John 15:11 - *"These things I have spoken to you, that my joy may be in you, and that your joy may be full."*

Psalm 16:11 - *"You make known to me the path of life; in your presence there is fullness of joy; at your right hand are pleasures forevermore."*

Philippians 4:4 - *"Rejoice in the Lord always; again I will say, rejoice."*

Romans 15:13 - *"May the God of hope fill you with all joy and peace in believing, so that by the power of the Holy Spirit you may abound in hope."*

Nehemiah 8:10 - *"Then he said to them, 'Go your way. Eat the fat and drink sweet wine and send portions to anyone who has nothing ready, for this day is holy to our Lord. And do not be grieved, for the joy of the Lord is your strength.'"*

Ephesians 2:10: *"For we are his workmanship, created in Christ Jesus for good works, which God prepared beforehand, that we should walk in them."*

Ephesians 1:4: *"Even as he chose us in him before the foundation of the world, that we should be holy and blameless before him. In love."*

Psalm 30:5 - *"For His anger is but for a moment, and His favor is for a lifetime. Weeping may tarry for the night, but joy comes with the morning."*

Psalm 94:19 - *"When the cares of my heart are many, Your consolations cheer my soul."*

Isaiah 61:10 - *"I will greatly rejoice in the Lord; my soul shall exult in my God, for He has clothed me with the garments of salvation; He has covered me with the robe of righteousness, as a bridegroom decks Himself like a priest with a beautiful headdress, and as a bride adorns herself with her jewels."*

Galatians 5:22-23 - *"But the fruit of the Spirit is love, joy, peace, patience, kindness, goodness, faithfulness, gentleness, self-control; against such things there is no law."*

Psalm 126:5 - *"Those who sow in tears shall reap with shouts of joy!"*

APPENDIX B: BIBLICAL TRUTHS TO COUNTER COMMON LIES
I Am Beautiful

The following powerful bible verses dispel the lie that I am ugly.

Psalm 139:14 - *"I praise you, for I am fearfully and wonderfully made. Wonderful are your works; my soul knows it very well."*

1 Samuel 16:7 - *"But the Lord said to Samuel, 'Do not look on his appearance or on the height of his stature, because I have rejected him. For the Lord sees not as man sees: man looks on the outward appearance, but the Lord looks on the heart.'"*

Proverbs 31:30 - *"Charm is deceitful, and beauty is vain, but a woman who fears the Lord is to be praised."*

1 Peter 3:3-4 - *"Do not let your adorning be external—the braiding of hair and the putting on of gold jewelry, or the clothing you wear—but let your adorning be the hidden person of the heart with the imperishable beauty of a gentle and quiet spirit, which in God's sight is very precious."*

Ephesians 2:10 - *"For we are his workmanship, created in Christ Jesus for good works, which God prepared beforehand, that we should walk in them."*

Song of Solomon 4:7 - *"You are altogether beautiful, my love; there is no flaw in you."*

Isaiah 43:4 - *"Because you are precious in my eyes, and honored, and I love you, I give men in return for you, peoples in exchange for your life."*

Romans 12:2 - *"Do not be conformed to this world, but be transformed by the renewal of your mind, that by testing you may discern what is the will of God, what is good and acceptable and perfect."*

1 Corinthians 6:19-20 - *"Or do you not know that your body is a temple of the Holy Spirit within you, whom you have from God? You are not your own, for you were bought with a price. So glorify God in your body."*

Psalm 45:11 - *"And the king will desire your beauty. Since he is your lord, bow to him."*

Song of Solomon 6:4 - *"You are beautiful as Tirzah, my love, lovely as Jerusalem, awesome as an army with banners."*

APPENDIX B: BIBLICAL TRUTHS TO COUNTER COMMON LIES

I Am Strong With God

The following powerful bible verses dispel the lie that I am weak.

Philippians 4:13 - *"I can do all things through him who strengthens me."*

2 Corinthians 12:9 - *"But he said to me, 'My grace is sufficient for you, for my power is made perfect in weakness.' Therefore I will boast all the more gladly of my weaknesses, so that the power of Christ may rest upon me."*

Isaiah 40:29 - *"He gives power to the faint, and to him who has no might He increases strength."*

Psalm 18:32 - *"the God who equipped me with strength and made my way blameless."*

Ephesians 6:10 - *"Finally, be strong in the Lord and in the strength of His might."*

Isaiah 41:10 - *" I will strengthen you, I will help you, I will uphold you with My righteous right hand."*

2 Timothy 1:7 - *"for God gave us a spirit not of fear but of power and love and self-control."*

Psalm 73:26 - *"My flesh and my heart may fail, but God is the strength of my heart and my portion forever."*

Psalm 18:39 - *"For you equipped me with strength for the battle; you made those who rise against me sink under me."*

Isaiah 40:28-31 - *"Have you not known? Have you not heard? The Lord is the everlasting God, the Creator of the ends of the earth. He does not faint or grow weary; his understanding is unsearchable. He gives power to the faint, and to him who has no might he increases strength. Even youths shall faint and be weary, and young men shall fall exhausted; but they who wait for the Lord shall renew their strength; they shall mount up with wings like eagles; they shall run and not be weary; they shall walk and not faint."*

APPENDIX B: BIBLICAL TRUTHS TO COUNTER COMMON LIES
My Past is Gone

The following bible verses dispel the lie that I am defined by my past.

2 Corinthians 5:17 - *"Therefore, if anyone is in Christ, he is a new creation. The old has passed away; behold, the new has come."*

Philippians 3:13-14 - *"Brothers, I do not consider that I have made it my own. But one thing I do: forgetting what lies behind and straining forward to what lies ahead, I press on toward the goal for the prize of the upward call of God in Christ Jesus."*

Isaiah 43:18-19 - *"Remember not the former things, nor consider the things of old. Behold, I am doing a new thing; now it springs forth, do you not perceive it? I will make a way in the wilderness and rivers in the desert."*

Romans 8:1 - *"There is therefore now no condemnation for those who are in Christ Jesus."*

Ephesians 4:22-24 - *"To put off your old self, which belongs to your former manner of life and is corrupt through deceitful desires, and to be renewed in the spirit of your minds, and to put on the new self, created after the likeness of God in true righteousness and holiness."*

Jeremiah 29:11 - *"For I know the plans I have for you, declares the Lord, plans for welfare and not for evil, to give you a future and a hope."*

Philippians 4:8 - *"Finally, brothers, whatever is true, whatever is honorable, whatever is just, whatever is pure, whatever is lovely, whatever is commendable, if there is any excellence, if there is anything worthy of praise, think about these things."*

1 John 1:9 - *"If we confess our sins, He is faithful and just to forgive us our sins and to cleanse us from all unrighteousness."*

Micah 7:19 - *"He will again have compassion on us; He will tread our iniquities underfoot. You will cast all our sins into the depths of the sea."*

Psalm 103:12 - *"As far as the east is from the west, so far does He remove our transgressions from us."*

APPENDIX B: BIBLICAL TRUTHS TO COUNTER COMMON LIES
I'm More Than Enough

The following powerful bible verses dispel the lie that I am not enough. I am more than enough because what I lack Jesus supplies.

Philippians 4:13 - *"I can do all things through him who strengthens me."*

2 Corinthians 3:5 - *"Not that we are sufficient in ourselves to claim anything as coming from us, but our sufficiency is from God,"*

Ephesians 2:10 - *"For we are his workmanship, created in Christ Jesus for good works, which God prepared beforehand, that we should walk in them."*

Psalm 139:14 - *"I praise you, for I am fearfully and wonderfully made. Wonderful are your works; my soul knows it very well."*

Colossians 2:9-10 - *"For in him the whole fullness of deity dwells bodily, and you have been filled in him, who is the head of all rule and authority."*

Romans 8:37 - *"No, in all these things we are more than conquerors through Him who loved us."*

2 Corinthians 12:9 - *"But He said to me, 'My grace is sufficient for you, for my power is made perfect in weakness.' Therefore I will boast all the more gladly of my weaknesses, so that the power of Christ may rest upon me."*

Psalm 46:1 - *"God is our refuge and strength, a very present help in trouble."*

Matthew 6:26 - *"Look at the birds of the air: they neither sow nor reap nor gather into barns, and yet your heavenly Father feeds them. Are you not of more value than they?"*

Philippians 1:6 - *"And I am sure of this, that He who began a good work in you will bring it to completion at the day of Jesus Christ."*

2 Corinthians 3:4 - *"Such is the confidence that we have through Christ toward God."*

Ephesians 3:16 - *"That according to the riches of his glory he may grant you to be strengthened with power through his Spirit in your inner being."*

1 Corinthians 1:27 - *"But God chose what is foolish in the world to shame the wise; God chose what is weak in the world to shame the strong."*

APPENDIX B: BIBLICAL TRUTHS TO COUNTER COMMON LIES
I'm Not a Burden

The following powerful bible verses dispel the lie that I am a burden.

Matthew 11:28-30 - *"Come to me, all who labor and are heavy laden, and I will give you rest. Take my yoke upon you, and learn from me, for I am gentle and lowly in heart, and you will find rest for your souls. For my yoke is easy, and my burden is light."*

Psalm 55:22 - *"Cast your burden on the Lord, and he will sustain you; he will never permit the righteous to be moved."*

1 Peter 5:7 - *"Casting all your anxieties on him, because He cares for you."*

Isaiah 41:10 - *"Fear not, for I am with you; be not dismayed, for I am your God; I will strengthen you, I will help you, I will uphold you with my righteous right hand."*

Romans 8:31 - *"What then shall we say to these things? If God is for us, who can be against us?"*

Psalm 68:19 - *"Blessed be the Lord, who daily bears us up; God is our salvation."*

Romans 15:1 - *"We who are strong have an obligation to bear with the failings of the weak, and not to please ourselves."*

Galatians 6:2 - *"Bear one another's burdens, and so fulfill the law of Christ."*

2 Corinthians 12:9-10 - *"But He said to me, 'My grace is sufficient for you, for my power is made perfect in weakness.' Therefore I will boast all the more gladly of my weaknesses, so that the power of Christ may rest upon me. For the sake of Christ, then, I am content with weaknesses, insults, hardships, persecutions, and calamities. For when I am weak, then I am strong."*

Matthew 6:26 - *"Look at the birds of the air: they neither sow nor reap nor gather into barns, and yet your heavenly Father feeds them. Are you not of more value than they?"*

APPENDIX B: BIBLICAL TRUTHS TO COUNTER COMMON LIES

I'm am Seen & Significant

The following powerful bible verses dispel the lie that I am invisible or insignificant.

Genesis 16:13 *"Then she called the name of the Lord who spoke to her, You-Are-the-God-Who-Sees; for she said, 'Have I also here seen Him who sees me?'*

Matthew 10:29-31 - *"Are not two sparrows sold for a penny? And not one of them will fall to the ground apart from your Father. But even the hairs of your head are all numbered. Fear not, therefore; you are of more value than many sparrows."*

Psalm 8:3-4 - *"When I look at Your heavens, the work of Your fingers, the moon and the stars, which You have set in place, what is man that You are mindful of him, and the son of man that you care for him?"*

Ephesians 1:4-5 - *"Even as he chose us in Him before the foundation of the world, that we should be holy and blameless before Him. In love He predestined us for adoption to Him as sons through Jesus Christ, according to the purpose of His will."*

Psalm 139:17-18 - *"How precious to me are Your thoughts, O God! How vast is the sum of them! If I would count them, they are more than the sand...."*

Isaiah 49:16 - *"Behold, I have engraved you on the palms of my hands; your walls are continually before me."*

Luke 12:6-7 - *"Are not five sparrows sold for two pennies? And not one of them is forgotten before God. Why, even the hairs of your head are all numbered. Fear not; you are of more value than many sparrows."*

Jeremiah 29:11 - *"For I know the plans I have for you, declares the Lord, plans for welfare and not for evil, to give you a future and a hope."*

Psalm 139:1-4 - *"O Lord, you have searched me and known me! You know when I sit down and when I rise up; you discern my thoughts from afar. You search out my path and my lying down and are acquainted with all my ways. Even before a word is on my tongue, behold, O Lord, you know it altogether."*

APPENDIX B: BIBLICAL TRUTHS TO COUNTER COMMON LIES
I Can Forgive With God's Grace

The following powerful bible verses dispel the lie that I will never be able to forgive.

Ephesians 4:32 - *"Be kind to one another, tenderhearted, forgiving one another, as God in Christ forgave you."*

Colossians 3:13 - *"Bearing with one another and, if one has a complaint against another, forgiving each other; as the Lord has forgiven you, so you also must forgive."*

Matthew 6:14-15 - *"For if you forgive others their trespasses, your heavenly Father will also forgive you, but if you do not forgive others their trespasses, neither will your Father forgive your trespasses."*

Mark 11:25 - *"And whenever you stand praying, forgive, if you have anything against anyone, so that your Father also who is in heaven may forgive you your trespasses."*

Luke 6:37 - *"Judge not, and you will not be judged; condemn not, and you will not be condemned; forgive, and you will be forgiven."*

Matthew 18:21-22 - *"Then Peter came up and said to him, 'Lord, how often will my brother sin against me, and I forgive him? As many as seven times?' Jesus said to him, 'I do not say to you seven times, but seventy-seven times.'"*

Luke 17:3-4 - *"Pay attention to yourselves! If your brother sins, rebuke him, and if he repents, forgive him, and if he sins against you seven times in the day, and turns to you seven times, saying, 'I repent,' you must forgive him."*

Ephesians 4:31-32 - *"Let all bitterness and wrath and anger and clamor and slander be put away from you, along with all malice. Be kind to one another, tenderhearted, forgiving one another, as God in Christ forgave you."*

Mark 11:25 - *"And whenever you stand praying, forgive, if you have anything against anyone, so that your Father also who is in heaven may forgive you your trespasses."*

APPENDIX B: BIBLICAL TRUTHS TO COUNTER COMMON LIES
God is Not Angry

The following powerful bible verses dispel the lie that God is angry at you. If you are a Christian you no longer have the wrath of God or His punishment.

Romans 5:9: *"Since, therefore, we have now been justified by His blood, much more shall we be saved by Him from the wrath of God."*

Isaiah 54:9-10 - *"'This is like the days of Noah to me: as I swore that the waters of Noah should no more go over the earth, so I have sworn that I will not be angry with you, and will not rebuke you. For the mountains may depart and the hills be removed, but my steadfast love shall not depart from you, and my covenant of peace shall not be removed,' says the Lord, who has compassion on you."*

Romans 8:1 - *"There is therefore now no condemnation for those who are in Christ Jesus."*

John 3:16-17 - *"For God did not send His Son into the world to condemn the world, but in order that the world might be saved through Him."*

1 John 4:10 - *"In this is love, not that we have loved God but that He loved us and sent his Son to be the propitiation for our sins."*

Ephesians 1:7-8 - *"In Him we have redemption through His blood, the forgiveness of our trespasses, according to the riches of His grace, which He lavished upon us, in all wisdom and insight."*

1 John 4:18 - *"There is no fear in love, but perfect love casts out fear. For fear has to do with punishment, and whoever fears has not been perfected in love."*

Colossians 1:21-22 - *"And you, who once were alienated and hostile in mind, doing evil deeds, He has now reconciled in His body of flesh by His death, in order to present you holy and blameless and above reproach before Him."*

John 5:24 - *"Truly, truly, I say to you, whoever hears my word and believes him who sent me has eternal life. He does not come into judgment, but has passed from death to life."*

APPENDIX C: GOING DEEPER
SPIRITUAL GIFTS: COMPLETE SCRIPTURE REFERENCES

Administration

1 Corinthians 12:28 *"And God has placed in the church first of all apostles, second prophets, third teachers, then miracles, then gifts of healing, of helping, of guidance, and of different kinds of tongues."*

Apostleship

1 Corinthians 12:28 *"And God has placed in the church first of all apostles, second prophets, third teachers, then miracles, then gifts of healing, of helping, of guidance, and of different kinds of tongues."*

Ephesians 4:11 *"So Christ himself gave the apostles, the prophets, the evangelists, the pastors and teachers,"*

Craftsmanship

Exodus 31:1-5 *"Then the Lord said to Moses, 'See, I have chosen Bezalel son of Uri, the son of Hur, of the tribe of Judah, and I have filled him with the Spirit of God, with wisdom, with understanding, with knowledge and with all kinds of skills—to make artistic designs for work in gold, silver and bronze, to cut and set stones, to work in wood, and to engage in all kinds of crafts.'"*

Exodus 35:30-35 *"Then Moses said to the Israelites, 'See, the Lord has chosen Bezalel son of Uri, the son of Hur, of the tribe of Judah, and he has filled him with the Spirit of God, with wisdom, with understanding, with knowledge and with all kinds of skills—to make artistic designs for work in gold, silver and bronze, to cut and set stones, to work in wood and to engage in all kinds of artistic crafts. And he has given both him and Oholiab son of Ahisamak, of the tribe of Dan, the ability to teach others. He has filled them with skill to do all kinds of work as engravers, designers, embroiderers in blue, purple and scarlet yarn and fine linen, and weavers—all of them skilled workers and designers.'"*

Discernment

1 Corinthians 12:10 *"to another miraculous powers, to another prophecy, to another distinguishing between spirits, to another speaking in different kinds of tongues, and to still another the interpretation of tongues."*

Hebrews 5:14 *"But solid food is for the mature, who by constant use have trained themselves to distinguish good from evil."*

Evangelism

Ephesians 4:11 *"So Christ himself gave the apostles, the prophets, the evangelists, the pastors and teachers,"*

2 Timothy 4:5 *"But you, keep your head in all situations, endure hardship, do the work of an evangelist, discharge all the duties of your ministry."*

APPENDIX C: GOING DEEPER

SPIRITUAL GIFTS: COMPLETE SCRIPTURE REFERENCES (CONTINUED)

Exhortation

Romans 12:8 *"if it is to encourage, then give encouragement; if it is giving, then give generously; if it is to lead, do it diligently; if it is to show mercy, do it cheerfully."*

Faith

1 Corinthians 12:9 *"to another faith by the same Spirit, to another gifts of healing by that one Spirit,"*

Giving

Romans 12:8 *"if it is to encourage, then give encouragement; if it is giving, then give generously; if it is to lead, do it diligently; if it is to show mercy, do it cheerfully."*

Healing

1 Corinthians 12:9 *"to another faith by the same Spirit, to another gifts of healing by that one Spirit,"*

1 Corinthians 12:28 *"And God has placed in the church first of all apostles, second prophets, third teachers, then miracles, then gifts of healing, of helping, of guidance, and of different kinds of tongues."*

Helps

1 Corinthians 12:28 *"And God has placed in the church first of all apostles, second prophets, third teachers, then miracles, then gifts of healing, of helping, of guidance, and of different kinds of tongues."*

Hospitality

1 Peter 4:9-10 *"Offer hospitality to one another without grumbling. Each of you should use whatever gift you have received to serve others, as faithful stewards of God's grace in its various forms."*

Romans 12:13 *"Share with the Lord's people who are in need. Practice hospitality."*

Intercession

Romans 8:26-27 *"In the same way, the Spirit helps us in our weakness. We do not know what we ought to pray for, but the Spirit himself intercedes for us through wordless groans. And he who searches our hearts knows the mind of the Spirit, because the Spirit intercedes for God's people in accordance with the will of God."*

1 Timothy 2:1-2 *"I urge, then, first of all, that petitions, prayers, intercession and thanksgiving be made for all people—for kings and all those in authority, that we may live peaceful and quiet lives in all godliness and holiness."*

Knowledge

1 Corinthians 12:8 *"To one there is given through the Spirit a message of wisdom, to another a message of knowledge by means of the same Spirit,"*

APPENDIX C: GOING DEEPER

SPIRITUAL GIFTS: COMPLETE SCRIPTURE REFERENCES (CONTINUED)

Leadership

Romans 12:8 *"if it is to encourage, then give encouragement; if it is giving, then give generously; if it is to lead, do it diligently; if it is to show mercy, do it cheerfully."*

Mercy

Romans 12:8 *"if it is to encourage, then give encouragement; if it is giving, then give generously; if it is to lead, do it diligently; if it is to show mercy, do it cheerfully."*

Miracles

1 Corinthians 12:10 *"to another miraculous powers, to another prophecy, to another distinguishing between spirits, to another speaking in different kinds of tongues, and to still another the interpretation of tongues."*

1 Corinthians 12:28 *"And God has placed in the church first of all apostles, second prophets, third teachers, then miracles, then gifts of healing, of helping, of guidance, and of different kinds of tongues."*

Pastoring/Shepherding

Ephesians 4:11 *"So Christ himself gave the apostles, the prophets, the evangelists, the pastors and teachers,"*

1 Peter 5:2-4 *"Be shepherds of God's flock that is under your care, watching over them—not because you must, but because you are willing, as God wants you to be; not pursuing dishonest gain, but eager to serve; not lording it over those entrusted to you, but being examples to the flock. And when the Chief Shepherd appears, you will receive the crown of glory that will never fade away."*

Prophecy

Romans 12:6 *"We have different gifts, according to the grace given to each of us. If your gift is prophesying, then prophesy in accordance with your faith."*

1 Corinthians 12:10 *"to another miraculous powers, to another prophecy, to another distinguishing between spirits, to another speaking in different kinds of tongues, and to still another the interpretation of tongues."*

1 Corinthians 14:1-5 *"Follow the way of love and eagerly desire gifts of the Spirit, especially prophecy. For anyone who speaks in a tongue does not speak to people but to God. Indeed, no one understands them; they utter mysteries by the Spirit. But the one who prophesies speaks to people for their strengthening, encouraging and comfort. Anyone who speaks in a tongue edifies themselves, but the one who prophesies edifies the church. I would like every one of you to speak in tongues, but I would rather have you prophesy. The one who prophesies is greater than the one who speaks in tongues, unless someone interprets, so that the church may be edified."*

APPENDIX C: GOING DEEPER

SPIRITUAL GIFTS: COMPLETE SCRIPTURE REFERENCES (CONTINUED)

Service

Romans 12:7 *"if it is serving, then serve; if it is teaching, then teach;"*

1 Peter 4:11 *"If anyone speaks, they should do so as one who speaks the very words of God. If anyone serves, they should do so with the strength God provides, so that in all things God may be praised through Jesus Christ. To him be the glory and the power for ever and ever. Amen.*

Teaching

Romans 12:7 *"if it is serving, then serve; if it is teaching, then teach;"*

1 Corinthians 12:28 *"And God has placed in the church first of all apostles, second prophets, third teachers, then miracles, then gifts of healing, of helping, of guidance, and of different kinds of tongues."*

Ephesians 4:11 *"So Christ himself gave the apostles, the prophets, the evangelists, the pastors and teachers,"*

Speaking in Tongues/Interpretation

1 Corinthians 12:10 *"to another miraculous powers, to another prophecy, to another distinguishing between spirits, to another speaking in different kinds of tongues, and to still another the interpretation of tongues."*

1 Corinthians 12:28 *"And God has placed in the church first of all apostles, second prophets, third teachers, then miracles, then gifts of healing, of helping, of guidance, and of different kinds of tongues."*

1 Corinthians 14:2-5 *"For anyone who speaks in a tongue does not speak to people but to God. Indeed, no one understands them; they utter mysteries by the Spirit. But the one who prophesies speaks to people for their strengthening, encouraging and comfort. Anyone who speaks in a tongue edifies themselves, but the one who prophesies edifies the church. I would like every one of you to speak in tongues, but I would rather have you prophesy. The one who prophesies is greater than the one who speaks in tongues, unless someone interprets, so that the church may be edified."*

1 Corinthians 14:13-19, 18-19 *"For this reason the one who speaks in a tongue should pray that they may interpret what they say. For if I pray in a tongue, my spirit prays, but my mind is unfruitful. [....] I thank God that I speak in tongues more than all of you. But in the church I would rather speak five intelligible words to instruct others than ten thousand words in a tongue."* (look up reference for full context)

Wisdom

1 Corinthians 12:8 *"To one there is given through the Spirit a message of wisdom, to another a message of knowledge by means of the same Spirit,"*

CONTINUE TO Learn From JESUS

www.ingramcontent.com/pod-product-compliance
Lightning Source LLC
Chambersburg PA
CBHW081130090426

42737CB00018B/3286